"*Only One Way?* guides us unerringly through the contemporary world of religious pluralism and points us to Jesus Christ alone as the Way, the Truth, and the Life. Grasping the central truth that the Christian gospel is unintelligible apart from the uniqueness of Christ, these pages expound it in a variety of insightful ways. Here are six scholars and pastors boldly upholding the only kind of Christianity worthy of the name. We should be thankful for each of them!"

—SINCLAIR B. FERGUSON, Senior Minister,
The First Presbyterian Church, Columbia, South Carolina

"Although religious pluralism is often treated as a 'postmodern' phenomenon, it has always been the world's most fundamental challenge to the gospel. The authors of this thoughtful work press us, as the apostles did, to stand against the world for the world's sake. Only one way? At a time when many evangelicals don't seem so sure these writers help us to confidently answer yes!"

—MICHAEL HORTON, Gresham Machen Professor of
Systematic Theology and Apologetics,
Westminster Seminary California, Escondido, California.

"There is a battle raging in the world today—it is a battle for truth. And in a day when the god of relativism governs hearts and minds throughout the world, Christians cannot be silent. This timely book calls God's people to action. I am thankful the Lord has raised up faithful men to stand firm and proclaim boldly the truth about God's truth. Amid all the confusion surrounding postmodernism and pluralism, this book clears the air. God's people will know where to turn as the Lord tears down strongholds and redirects the world to the Way, the Truth, and the Life."

—BURK PARSONS, Editor of *Tabletalk* magazine;
Minister of Congregational Life, Saint Andrew's Chapel,
Sanford, Florida.

Only One Way?

Only One Way?

Reaffirming the Exclusive Truth Claims of Christianity

Edited by RICHARD D. PHILLIPS

CROSSWAY BOOKS

A PUBLISHING MINISTRY OF
GOOD NEWS PUBLISHERS
WHEATON, ILLINOIS

Only One Way? Reaffirming the Exclusive Truth Claims of Christianity
Copyright © 2006 by The Alliance of Confessing Evangelicals
Published by Crossway Books
    a publishing ministry of Good News Publishers
    1300 Crescent Street
    Wheaton, Illinois 60187

Cover design: Josh Dennis

Cover photo: Getty Images

First printing 2007

Printed in the United States of America

ISBN 13: 978-1-58134-801-9

ISBN 10: 1-58134-801-0

Library of Congress Cataloging-in-Publication Data
Phillips, Richard D. (Richard Davis), 1960–
Only One Way? Reaffirming the Exclusive Truth Claims of Christianity /
Richard D. Phillips
    p. cm.
    Includes bibliographical references and index.
    ISBN 13: 978-1-58134-801-9 (tpb)
    1. Apologetics. I. Title.
BT1103.P48   2006
239—dc22   2006026380

VP		16	15	14	13	12	11	10	09	08	07
14	13	12	11	10	9	8	7	6	5	4	3	2

To Him

*Who is the Way, the Truth,
and the Life.* —JOHN 14:6

Contents

Contributors

David F. Wells. Andrew Mutch Distinguished Professor of Historical and Systematic Theology, Gordon-Conwell Theological Seminary, South Hamilton, Massachusetts.

Peter R. Jones. Director, Christian Witness to a Pagan Planet; Adjunct Professor and Scholar-in-Residence, Westminster Seminary California, Escondido, California.

Richard D. Phillips. Senior Minister, First Presbyterian Church, Coral Springs, Florida.

Philip G. Ryken. Senior Minister, Tenth Presbyterian Church, Philadelphia, Pennsylvania.

J. Ligon Duncan III. Senior Minister, First Presbyterian Church, Jackson, Mississippi.

D. A. Carson. Research Professor of New Testament, Trinity Evangelical Divinity School, Deerfield, Illinois.

Preface

A major shift is taking place in the consciousness of Western civilization, a shift that greatly impacts the Christian church. This shift is known as the movement from *modernity* to *postmodernity*. Modernity was proud, confident, and certain. But its postmodern stepchild is marked by despair, suspicion, and confusion. Some Christians have hailed postmodernity as a breath of fresh air in which the Holy Spirit's hand may be perceived—a refreshing sign of repentance from the sins of modernity. But at least one feature of postmodernity—in fact, a central feature—is its espousal of relativism in matters of truth. So what happens to the exclusive claims of the Christian faith in such an environment? Can we—should we—continue to assert that ours is the one truth from heaven? Is it still necessary to worship only the Christian expression of God? Can we really continue to insist that Jesus is the only Savior, apart from whom we must perish under God's wrath?

The contributors to this book are convinced that Christians can continue to affirm the exclusive claims of the biblical message, indeed, that we must defend especially these claims if we are to communicate effectively the biblical gospel to a postmodern world. As Philip Ryken asserts: "For all its insights, postmodernism must be recognized as an attack on the very foundations of truth, and we must join the battle at the very place where truth is under attack" (p. 92).

The six chapters of this book follow a general progression. The introductory chapter by David Wells locates us with the apostle Paul in the pagan Athens of Acts 17. If there has ever been a time since the Reformation when Christians find themselves in a situation like Paul's Athens, that time is now. Peter Jones follows in chapter 2 by noting that at its foundation, neo-pagan postmodernism involves a rejection of the biblical idea of God himself. Both Wells and Jones warn Christians—and especially evangelists and apologists—of our great need to understand the intellectual and spiritual environment of our time. Both perceive a threat as well as an opportunity for a biblically faithful and intellectually credible Christian witness to the postmodern age.

The middle two chapters tackle specific topics that are under siege by the world and are also in danger of abandonment by postmodern-minded Christians. Chapter 3 (my chapter) considers the biblical claim of Jesus Christ as the world's only Savior. Can we continue to insist that people must believe on Jesus Christ—and him only—in order to be saved? What is the biblical basis for such a claim? Why is this such a hotly contested doctrine? Philip Ryken then confronts us in chapter 4 with Pontius Pilate's unforgettable question, posed to Jesus himself during the Roman trial: "What is truth?" (John 18:38). Is there one truth from God, or must we agree that there are as many truths as there are perspectives?

The book concludes with two chapters directed not so much to the conflict of ideas between Christianity and the world, but to the Christian's own embrace of the Bible's call to exclusivity. In Chapter 5, Ligon Duncan reflects on the "one people" united through faith in Jesus Christ. If we are to be a people of truth, we must together be the people we are called to be. Lastly, in chapter 6, D. A. Carson ponders whether this exclusivity penetrates to the living of our lives. Is there "one way" in which Christians must live? If so, what is it, and how can people like us ever hope to fulfill it?

This material originated as conference addresses to the 2005 Philadelphia Conference on Reformed Theology (PCRT), sponsored by the Alliance of Confessing Evangelicals, and this book is published as a partnership between the Alliance and Crossway Books. We chose the theme, *One Way*, because of our mission to promote "clarity and conviction about the great evangelical truths of the gospel and to proclaim these truths powerfully in our contemporary context." I would like to express my sincere appreciation to Robert Brady, executive vice president of the Alliance of Confessing Evangelicals, and to our wonderful staff—especially those who work so hard to put on this historic conference year after year. I also thank Allan Fisher and all his colleagues at Crossway Books, not only for their hard work on this volume but for all their stalwart labors to advance the gospel. Lastly, I join with all the contributors in asking God for his richest blessings on all who consider what we have written, that faith might be renewed and strength be added to all who love the Lord Jesus Christ, who is the one Way, the one Truth, and the one Life (John 14:6). To him be glory forever.

Richard D. Phillips
Coral Springs, Florida

1

One Among Many

DAVID F. WELLS

The God who made the world and everything in it, being Lord of heaven and earth, does not live in temples made by man, nor is he served by human hands, as though he needed anything, since he himself gives to all mankind life and breath and everything.

ACTS 17:24–25

That our world has been engulfed by change is indisputable. Some of these changes, in fact, have transformed our world's shape and they have also massively increased our ability to act in it.

Let me offer but one illustration. My father was born in 1898. When he was a young man (actually below the legal age) he joined the cavalry and was trained to serve with the British forces in World War I. He was shipped out to Palestine. In 1916, he was part of history's last successful sword charge. The cavalry, in fact, was rapidly being rendered obsolete by an invention which had just made its debut: the machine gun. This invention was to change the way war was waged and it was only one of many innovations that were to follow. And this is the point. Within the span of little more than one lifetime, in fact, we have come from fighting with the sword to using the high technology weaponry that we've seen on our television screens in the two Iraq wars. Within one lifetime, we have moved from that earlier hand-to-hand combat to the use of cameras in bomb noses, smart bombs, guided missiles, night goggles, computers in tanks, and the unbelievable escalation in the sheer destructive capabilities that we now possess. All of this has happened in less than one century!

When we add to this the many other kinds of change which happened in the twentieth century—and the many kinds of change which happened in every century before it—we realize that as soon as we start traveling back in time, we quickly find ourselves in a world and a time that is quite unlike our own. There are no cars, TVs or video equipment, no aspirin, antibiotics or surgery, no movies, video pornography, or white collar identity theft, no public transportation or airliners, no air conditioning, heating, or oil deliveries, no birth control pills, no hospitals, no insurance policies, no retirement accounts, and no Social Security. This, in fact, is the world in which the apostle Paul lived, and in so many respects it is different from our own. This being the case, we may well ask how anything that he wrote, or any apologetic which he launched, could have any bearing on our world and the issues that we face.

This, of course, was the frequently stated argument among the churchmen and theologians of liberal Protestantism. The modern world, they said, had progressed so far that it was threatening to leave Christianity behind in its dust. Without assiduous updates, biblical Christianity would soon be rendered obsolete and outdated, a kind of pitiful brontosaurus that was doomed for extinction.

The liberals were right on one point. It is true that the world has undergone massive, breathtaking changes. But what they overlooked was the fact that in the midst of all of this change, some things have not changed at all. God in his character, counsels, and knowledge has not changed; the human being, though fallen, remains in the image of God; sin in its nature has not changed across the ages; the significance of God's acts in history has not changed; the abiding truth of God's word has not changed; the reality of the incarnation and the results of the cross have not changed, so neither has the gospel. It is the same gospel which is to be believed in all places and times, and among every tribe, ethnic group, culture, and generation. It is no different today for those in the Builder generation than for those who are Baby Boomers, or Gen Xers, or those in the Millennial generation, though you would never guess this from listening to the more adventurous, entrepreneurial evangelical leaders who are busy growing their own churches in selected generational niches.

The revelation God has given us in his Word is enduring in its relevance, in all places and times, precisely because it corresponds to what does not change. It is not simply a reflection of the changing culture of a world long since vanished, the cultural worlds in which it first arose. It is God's truth for the church in all ages and all seasons.

This is a little distinction which postmoderns typically do not understand. They think that there is no abiding truth, that all "truths" are the product of their own social environment and therefore never have any more than a local or personal applicability. Truth for one person may be quite different from truth for another. Not only so, but there are many in the evangelical world who are, perhaps in a different way, so captivated by the whirl of contemporary change, so busy fashioning the church in the emerging postmodern light on the fallacious assumption, that there are few, if any, realities in life that are enduring and unchanging—that they, too, are in danger of ending up with a purely individualized sense of truth. Why would they do this?

The reason, I believe, is that the fascination with what is changing is proving more compelling than considerations about what is not changing, and what is in flux seems to offer a more immediate access to the postmodern soul than what is stable. The problem, of course, is that so many in the postmodern world have become addicts to change and their appetite for it is no panacea for the gospel. It is in the soil of our bored lives that fads and fashions sprout, each one suggesting something new, something different, something that is riding the crest of a wave of what is "in," or some new potential for us just coming into sight. This is true, not only of cars and clothes, music and hangouts, but of belief and behavior, too. The adaptations which so many evangelicals are willing to make to this mood, I believe, are adaptations, not to what is innocent and inevitable, but to what is sick and deformed. These postmodern proclivities should be challenged, not weakly accepted.

It may be, then, that our current infatuations with what is slick and breathtakingly *au courant* might lead us to wonder whether Paul's address on Mars Hill has anything to say to the twenty-first century in which we are now living since it arose in a world that disappeared long ago. After all, is it not the case that their issues were so different from ours as to be almost incomprehensible now to those of us who live in the Western, postmodern, highly urbanized, commercialized, video-saturated, and hyped-up world?

Besides the many realities in the nature of God as well as in human nature, which have not changed, let me begin, in answering this question, by suggesting two additional important points of connection between Paul's world and our own which may help us to see with fresh understanding the pertinence of his apologetic. These additional connections are important to see because they enable us to grasp the fact that his apologetic, although developed a long time ago, is actually addressed to a world that is not as different from our own as may have appeared at first sight. In fact, what Paul said stands as a remarkable model for how we should be addressing our own postmodern world, which is urbanized and full of religious pluralism and relativism. Today, Christ is only one among many—but that is the exact situation that Paul addressed at Mars Hill.

Paul's World and Ours

One snapshot that I want to look at from this ancient time is the picture that we have of Athens on the day Paul made his stand before its intellectuals on Mars Hill. Two things stand out about it. I want to describe these briefly and then note the parallels with our own world.

First is *urbanization*. Athens was obviously a great cosmopolitan city that drew people like a magnet. They evidently came from many places. Some also came from far away. This city was the crown jewel of the Greek world, renowned for its intellectual traditions, its eclectic atmosphere, and its artistic accomplishments. Perhaps most remarkable of all was the Acropolis, some of it still standing to this day, which was visible from about forty miles away. Yet this was by no means the only spectacular aspect to the city. On all sides, Athens was a city of great cultural accomplishment, and it drew people from across the then-known world. On the day when Paul took his stand in this city, there were foreigners present (Acts 17:21) mingling in the marketplace, and among the philosophical adherents present, Luke notes, were the Epicureans and Stoics (17:18).

One of the curiosities Luke notes was that the people of Athens spent their time in nothing except telling or hearing something new (17:21). How trivial, we may think! And how strange! Here was a city renowned for the depth of its intellectual life apparently infatuated with what was on the surface, with what was ephemeral and so often inconsequential.

However, it is worth pondering the fact that in this respect Athens was a notable forerunner of what is a pervasive reality today throughout the West. We are also busy satisfying the same insatiable yearning for novelty. We do it in different ways and on a scale that would have made these ancient Athenians drool! The appetite for knowing what is new in the world is partly satisfied by the evening news carried on NBC, ABC, CBS, CNN, and Fox in

America and other news organizations elsewhere in the West such as the BBC—programs that not only inform us as to what has happened, which is perfectly legitimate, but often do so in a way that tweaks and piques our interest in novelty itself. We quickly get bored unless the news items are constantly changing. And every week all Western societies are deluged beneath the flood of magazines that make a living out of touting, sometimes even fabricating, what is new, fashionable and "hot." The temptation, therefore, to think that these Athenians must have been very superficial people to be so interested in what is new and hot, needs to be tempered by the realization that our judgment of them has far-reaching applications on ourselves as well!

What we see in Athens, in fact, was really just a foretaste of what was to come in our world in ways far more numerous than simply that of novelty. For example, and far more important, while there have been cities in the world going back into the mists of time, urbanization has become one of the signature marks of our time. What is new is not the fact of cities. What is different about this modern development is, first, the number of people who are now living in cities as a percentage of the population and, second, the size of those cities. In 1999, for the first time ever, more people lived in cities worldwide than did not. In 1999, then, we moved from a world that had been predominantly rural to one that is now predominantly urban. Now, the world's dominant social organization is that of the city; today cities of ten million and more are no longer considered remarkable. The threshold of what qualifies as a large city has moved to twenty million and upwards!

What we see in Paul's Athens is what has become common and typical in our own cities. Cities draw large numbers of people into close proximity with each other. People of different ethnicities, worldviews, religions, cultural habits and mores are forced to live side-by-side. It is in this enforced rubbing of shoulders that the edges tend to be taken off the distinctiveness of all belief systems.

Cities tend to produce a kind of coerced civility. This civility may have good aspects, but more commonly it is bad. It is good if it diminishes the kind of bellicosity that diminishes people's ability to live in proximity without harm. It is bad when it produces such tolerance that belief systems are considered true only for the adherents. This, of course, is what has happened throughout the West, as all beliefs have felt the pull to concede to the pressures of relativism. Tolerance, in other words, is a virtue as applied to behavior, but it can be a vice when it surfaces in belief.

Those of us who are married are only too keenly aware of how much we have depended on the virtue of our spouses in showing kindness, patience, and consideration toward us as we stumble through life sometimes in unhappy ways. In short, we are dependent on them to exercise this beautiful virtue of tolerance. Without their tolerance in this sense, we would be doomed!

However, tolerance in the contemporary sense, which is pervasive throughout the West and almost demanded in our multi-cultural, religiously diverse societies, spells the end to historic Christianity. Paul faced this same ideological threat at Athens. Recognizing the same religious pluralism with which Western Christians are faced today, he refused to trim his message of truth to fit into that context.

Secondly, Athens was a city of great *idolatry*. Today, some of the remnants of the Athenians' gods and goddesses are still visible on the Acropolis but, in Paul's day, there were many additional deities scattered throughout the city. It was said that there were as many deities as people in Athens, and certainly the main ones were all present and worshiped, such as Neptune, Bacchus, Mercury, Jupiter, and Venus. The city, Luke tells us, was "full of idols" (17:16). His language suggests a kind of wild, uncontrolled, cancerous growth. Here were gods and goddesses proliferating in every direction, on every corner, holding sway—indeed, holding court!—over the whole city. No part of it was immune to their presence. These superstitions were, from Paul's perspective, like a dreadful pall that hung over the entire population. The Athenians, he said as he began his address, were "in every way . . . very religious" (17:22). He said that he had observed their objects of worship. This included one altar that apparently sought to cover any bases otherwise left uncovered, with its ascription to "the unknown god" (17:23).

Everybody in that ancient world knew about Athens, and no doubt Paul had heard about this city from the time he was a small boy. When he arrived there on this occasion, it would have been very natural for him to be as awed by what he saw as we might be today on visiting Paris or Venice for the first time. Indeed, Paul apparently did exactly what we typically do when visiting a large city. He walked around it taking in the sights. What were his impressions? What struck him most?

It would not have been unreasonable to think that what struck Paul was the greatness of Athenian culture. Its art, architecture, and intellectual life were renowned. Athens was at the very center of ancient learning. And Paul was no country bumpkin who was unable to appreciate these achievements. He was, in fact, a sophisticated, traveled, learned person of wide acquaintance and brilliant intellect. It would have been very natural for a person of his depth, as he wandered the streets of Athens, to find his breath being taken away.

Perhaps this did happen, but Luke tells us nothing along these lines. What he does record is not Paul's awe but the disturbance which happened in his spirit over the sight of all the idol worship. He was inwardly "provoked" in spirit, Luke tells us (17:16). It is, indeed, the same language as is typically used of God's own revulsion over idolatry in which the human need to worship is misdirected toward lifeless substitutes for God himself. What ignorance it is to suppose that these idols possessed eternal life, ruled providentially in this world, and could meet the deep needs that suffuse the human spirit in this fallen world!

Paul's own revulsion, however, was not simply over human miscalculation, error, and foolishness. It was, far more profoundly, about the fact that what should have been ascribed to God alone was being ascribed to human creations. God was being robbed of his glory. His glory, as it were, was being handed around to these humanly made artifacts that were being invested with powers they could never have and that were God's alone. That was what so provoked Paul.

This situation of proliferating, tangible idols may seem quite remote to sophisticated Westerners today, who have long since grown out of primitive beliefs like these. So it may seem. There is, however, an argument for saying that despite all of our intellectual sophistication we are returning to a situation that is not unlike what Paul faced.

One of the truly startling developments of the last few decades has been the resurfacing, throughout the West, of a spirituality that has many connections with the kind of paganism that Paul confronted. Tangible idols are not worshiped in today's spirituality, but so many of its assumptions, nevertheless, are still pagan.

In America, 78 percent say that they are spiritual, but half of these immediately add that though they are spiritual, they are not religious. By *religion* what they apparently mean is that they do not subscribe to any doctrines that have been passed on to them and that are not self-generated, to any corporate practice of their beliefs, or to ethical norms with which they themselves do not agree. On the grounds that they have God "within" them, 60 percent of Americans say that they do not need church. They are spiritual but not religious. And by spiritual, what they have in mind is some kind of mysterious access to an unseen power and this, many feel, has nothing to do with "religion." It is no surprise, then, that George Barna has found that when it comes to spiritual satisfaction, only 7 percent of Americans find it in the Bible, only 6 percent in helping others, only 1 percent in other believers, and only 3 percent in God (presumably the God of traditional Christianity). In life's crises, 56 percent say, they look for help from the power within, rather than to the God without, the God of religion. This pattern of surging spirituality which is largely antithetical to organized religion is evident throughout the West, not just in America.

It is not hard to see that this spirituality is quintessentially postmodern. It is spirituality that is self-generated, self-defined, subject to no outside authority, intensely therapeutic, unabashedly pragmatic, itself a testimony both to the fact that, as Augustine reminded us, our hearts are restless until they find their rest in God, and to the fact that in today's world with all of its complexity and pain, so many people are simply lost. They are anxiously reaching out for Something larger than themselves that will offer some solace, meaning, and mystery. At the same time, while this new spirituality is undoubtedly postmodern, it is also quite pagan. This is especially evident in its confusion between the searcher and the sacred, the creature and the Creator. This kind of pantheism was at the heart of all paganism. It is once again being heard in the voices of those Americans who say that inasmuch as they have God "within" they do not need the church, and that in life's crises they look to the power "within" for help, not to the God of traditional Christian faith. This is extremely close to what Paul himself encountered on that day in Athens when he confronted the reigning worldviews of his time.

It is, then, rather striking that despite the passage of the years, Paul's apologetic requires very little adaptation to our own contemporary situation. We begin where he did. We begin with the same God, the same Christ, the same human nature, the same sin, the same truth, and the same gospel. Furthermore, we are bringing all of this into a world which in some profound ways is like his, too. Our world is multiplying cities like the Athens of Paul's day. Here, today, are cities that draw people of every variety—of many races and ethnic groups, of all kinds of beliefs and behaviors—into close proximity with one another. The "marketplace" Luke mentions in Athens functioned much like the workplace in our modern cities. This enforced proximity to one another almost inevitably produces a climate of religious pluralism. The difference between the religious pluralism of Paul's day and of ours is less one of nature and more one of scale. Whereas in the Roman world there were few cities like Athens and relatively few who lived in cities, today there are many cities like Athens and a high percentage who live in them.

The resurgence of the new spirituality, even in the midst of the secularized cultures of the West, may seem to be breathlessly advanced, but it is, I am suggesting, so ancient as to be little different from what Paul encountered. The gods and goddesses may have disappeared, but the confusion between the spiritual searcher and the sacred is as evident as it was in the paganism of Paul's day. We would do well, then, to pay heed not only to what Paul said in his address but, just as importantly, to how he went about meeting his pagan contemporaries intellectually, for his experiences are, in many ways, ours.

Paul's Apologetic

The three recorded missionary addresses of Paul in Acts (13:16–41; 14:15–17; 17:16–33) are interesting for many reasons, but not least for how they show his sensitivity to his audience. In the first, for example, he was speaking to Jews and God-fearers, so it was natural that he would appeal to the biblical narrative with which they were so familiar. In Athens, however, his audience was quite different and would have had no idea what he was talking about. The only literary appeal Paul therefore made was to an unnamed Greek poet, presumably familiar to his audience, who had said that "In him we live and move and have our being" (Acts 17:28). There was no commonly owned authority to which Paul could appeal, so this was not where he started.

Luke, of course, has provided us with only a bare, brief summary of Paul's points and there is much that we might like to know that is omitted from his sparse account. How was Paul so familiar with the views of his audience? When did he study their philosophies? How long did he speak on this occasion? Was he interrupted? How did he flesh out each of the points Luke records? We do not know. What we can reasonably surmise, though, is that this address, which we have in summary form, and which can be read in a matter of minutes, was originally much longer. Yet even the summary we have is sufficient for us to see that Paul's foundational point of engagement with his audience dealt with the matter of worldviews.

On that day, Paul might have begun with a simple gospel message, but he did not. In fact, it is only at the very end of the address that we hear for the first time the issues of repentance (17:30), divine judgment, and the resurrection of Christ (17:31). This must seem rather startling to us. Rarely do we do what Paul did. Our inclination is to get the audience to the gospel in the shortest possible time and to the gospel in its most stripped-down version. If inquirers have questions, they come later, not at the beginning. Paul, however, was different. Before speaking about Christ and the gospel, he spoke about worldviews.

The reason for this seems rather clear. Jews who heard Paul's gospel were people well prepared by the Old Testament in their understanding about the nature of God and his relation to the creation, his holiness, the reality and consequences of sin, and the necessity of sacrifice. The pagans to whom Paul spoke were at sea in all of these matters. It was therefore important to Paul that the matter of worldview be confronted first. Otherwise, the gospel might well have been absorbed into a false worldview in which its nature and uniqueness might well be lost. The gospel, after all, is not a disembodied message which can be assimilated into just any worldview. Rather, it comes within its own understanding of the world, outside of which the gospel makes no sense at all. It is true that without believing the gospel, Paul's hearers would not know the God from whom they were alienated because of their sin and God's righteous indignation against that sin. It is also the case, however, that without an understanding of God as creator and judge, Paul's hearers could not understand the gospel. It is, there-fore, to the Christian God that Paul takes his hearers first, and he takes them there before he takes them to the gospel. What he argued for were three main defining characteristics in the reality of God, characteristics which also define how we should view our own world.[1]

The Creator God

Paul began his apologetic with what may seem like a conventional point: God "made the world and everything in it" (17:24). In so saying, he established a distinction between the Creator and cre-ation, between the One who makes and what is made. We do not know how, on this occasion, he elaborated on this distinction but we can say with certainty that if he drove home this distinction he did so in ways that reasserted truths from the Old Testament reve-lation. God, Paul said, "does not need anything" but instead "gives to all mankind life and breath and everything" (17:26). The world, in other words, is entirely dependent upon God for its life; he is not dependent on the world for his. God is independent, self-sufficient, and self-existent, whereas the life of the world is derived, borrowed, and dependent on him. This is how we should see matters. The

---

[1] Some of the material in this chapter is drawn from my book, *Above All Earthly Powers: Christ in the Postmodern World* (Grand Rapids: Eerdmans, 2005). I am also indebted to D. A. Carson, "Athens Revisited," in *Telling the Truth: Evangelizing Postmoderns*, ed. D. A. Carson (Grand Rapids: Zondervan, 2000), 384–98.

world has no existence apart from God; he, however, does have existence apart from the world.

Every form of paganism rested, in one way or another, on a pantheistic view of reality. This view is what Paul, in these brief recorded statements, demolished. In one stroke, he laid low all pagan ideas about sacred reality being infused in matter, matter as transmitting that sacred reality, or the Creator and creation as being indistinct from each other in important ways. God is the source of all that there is, Paul insisted. What exists outside of himself is different from him and exists, not on its own account, but as it is sustained by him.

This would have been quite startling to pagan ears. In their view, the gods and goddesses were quite dependent on humans. They were incomplete, sometimes lonely, sometimes needing humans for their plans, for the exercise of their whims and fancies, and even for their sexual satisfaction. In this ancient world, the deities were quite pint-sized, filled with human weaknesses, foibles, and needs. The biblical God, by contrast, is not. He needs nothing; he is complete in himself.

I would be negligent not to notice the strange parallel that now exists between the views Paul is here rejecting and the views that have surfaced in recent years among proponents of open theism such as Clark Pinnock, Greg Boyd, and John Sanders. Their views have made substantial inroads into a number of denominations. Pinnock has boasted that a majority in the evangelical world sides with him, and he could well be right.

So what are the open theists arguing? In their minds, they are protecting human freedom by arguing that God cannot know the future. Otherwise we would not be free in the moment of choice to do other than what we wanted to do. At the very last moment we could not change our minds if God, in advance, thought we were going to do something else. If we were able to change our minds, and God had thought we were going to do something different, he would be guilty of harboring false knowledge and imagining it to be true. To be free, therefore, open theism teaches that our actions must be hidden from God until we actually act. So, he does not know the future in its totality. His knowledge is just good guess-work. If the God of the open theists is in some respects complete, he is also quite lacking in other respects.

God needs us, we are told, to bring the creation project to a conclusion as his co-workers, and he needs us too to assuage his loneliness. God is not fully complete in himself in wisdom, power, and knowledge. This kind of divine insufficiency, this lack in the center of the God of open theism, I need to say, owes nothing to biblical thinking and everything to philosophies that are remote from biblical truth, indeed, as remote as paganism itself. But contrary to Pinnock's claim that God's self-sufficiency is an idea that Christians have borrowed from Aristotle, it is in fact the teaching of Paul before his pagan audience. For evangelicalism to survive in our neo-pagan world, we must not shrink back from the biblical idea of God on which Paul insists, not capitulating to the compromised vision of God offered by the open theists.

The Sovereign God

The second aspect of God's nature that Paul spoke about was his sovereignty. God is "Lord of heaven and earth" (17:24). It is no surprise to hear Paul spelling this out in terms of God directing the whole course of human history in accordance with his will, "having determined allotted periods and the boundaries of their dwelling place" (17:26) for every nation on earth. It is important to remember that this assertion of God's sovereignty was not simply an "in house" theological point that Paul was making. It actually cut right to the heart of the pagan impulse in two main ways.

First, this universal sovereignty distinguished the God of the Bible from every pagan god and goddess. Their "sovereignty," such as it was, was always local. Pagan deities ruled merely over this circumstance or that, this city or that, in this moment or in that. They ruled over a river, a field, in the ocean, in warfare, or at parties, but their rule was always partial, almost unpredictable, and often capricious. They, like us, were subject to bad moods and bad days. They, too, woke up on the wrong side of the bed, and sometimes their actions were irrational and incomprehensible. Not so the God of the Bible! His rule is universal and his actions are always predictable in the sense that they are defined by, and are the outgrowth of, God's unchanging holy character. As a result, his actions are always consistent with each other. That is why the theology of the Old Testament was very largely a theology of recitation—that is, of rehearsing the actions of God in the past because these actions offered strength, encouragement, and hope for the future. His actions in the past, they knew, carried within them the blueprint for what he would do in the future. God's redemptive plan is running its course through time, and nothing in all of life is ever an impediment to the realization of his sovereign, righteous will. In contrast to the very pagan idea of deity, God is the Lord of heaven and earth.

Secondly, this sovereignty is realized in matters of salvation. In Luke's account Paul does not draw this connection other than to declare that God is Lord, or sovereign, over the earth—and that surely includes matters of salvation. Later on in his address, he goes on to speak, as we shall see, of God's role in judging the earth and of the need for repentance and belief. These matters are not explicitly related to the working of his sovereign, saving will, but it takes little imagination for us to be able to connect the dots that Luke has given us, and which Paul may very well have specified in his total address.

Paul understood how different is the pagan approach to salvation from the biblical gospel. When it came to receiving benefits from the gods and goddesses, everything was based on a *quid pro quo*. They had to be approached, appeased, and satisfied through offerings and sacrifices—even child sacrifices. It was, at the crudest level, a kind of business deal. The actions of gods and worshipers were in reciprocal relation to one another. The pagan deities responded to what humans did. In this sense, pagan worshipers influenced the gods: it was the worshiper who tried to determine outcomes by what he or she did. In this way, bad moods in the deities could be deflected, their wrath averted, or their blessings secured.

It is because of this pagan context that some translators of the New Testament have been wary of using the language of propitiation where it seems to be demanded by the text. Not only does this word declare that there is kindled in the being of God a wrath whose outcome will be destructive, but it seems to suggest, along pagan lines, that human beings can take actions that will prevent this wrath from breaking out. This, critics say, is entirely inconsistent with the thinking found in the New Testament.

However, it is a mistake to abandon the language of propitiation. It should be used, but understood in its own biblical context. In the Bible it is God, not the worshiper, who provides the propitiation by which his own wrath is averted (Rom. 3:25; cf: 1 John 2:2; 4:10). There is never any thought of a business deal here—a bribe, a *quid pro quo*, or the sinner doing something that changes the mind of God. God does not negotiate or "deal" with sinners. God needs nothing from them and is under no obligation to them. Quite the reverse! It is they who are under his rule. It is he who provides salvation, and he provides it, not on their terms, but on his. He is the Lord, and his gift of salvation is received from him only as he offers it. He is sovereign and men are not. He rules and they are subject to his rule.

God the Judge

Toward the end of this address, we come to the place where Paul is about to speak of Christ and the gospel. There is, though, another and third piece in the doctrine of God that still needs to be dropped into place. It concerns God's moral nature. God, Paul said, "has fixed a day on which he will judge the world in righteousness" (Acts 17:31). This, too, was a startling thought.

That there was a single norm of righteousness, sustained by the character of God, was as unknown in the paganism of Paul's day as it is rapidly becoming unknown in our postmodern West. The gods and goddesses did not always behave morally, and the existence of multiple spheres of sacred influence, with all of their competing claims and agendas, only reinforced the idea that there is no single norm. Certainly, it was evident in this city given over to idolatry: there was obviously no single deity whose norm it was. They might just as well have said, in the language current in postmodern circles today, that there are no metanarratives remaining, no ultimate structures of meaning which are the same for everyone, for that is what they meant. The truth is that both paganism and postmodernity, for different reasons, nevertheless end up at the same place, and that is one of complete relativism.

Paul's claim, therefore, cut right across the bows of all paganism, just as it does our postmodern world. There is indeed a single, overarching Story, Paul insists, a structure of meaning that is the same for all people in all places and times, because the God whose "story" it is, is one God. In the presence of this Story, all of our small personal stories, all of our efforts to spin and fabricate meaning apart from him, are called into question. It is the character of God that asserts itself in his judgment, and it is before that divine being, in all of his holiness, that all are summoned.

Paul's Gospel in Athens

It is now rather evident how Paul has set up the structure of understanding without which the gospel would either have been incomprehensible or would have been perverted. Before speaking of this gospel, he has led his audience to consider the fact that God is their Creator and is independent of the creation. This means that there is no way in which he can be accessed intuitively from within creation or through the self, as if the sacred were in some way met within the self. God stands in a relation of complete independence from the creation, though Paul also did not want this to be misunderstood as if he were espousing a deistic understanding. No, given the fact that all people are the recipients of his general, nonsaving providence, "they should seek God, in the hope that they might feel their way toward him and find him" (17:27).

The point that Paul was making in asserting God's self-sufficiency was simply that God is separate from his creation. That, however, does not mean that he is remote or absent from life. We should note, however, that it is impossible that Paul was thinking that pagans might find this God in their own way, on their own terms, unless he was guilty of serious contradiction. After all, in Romans Paul argues that given the impulses of sin, "no one seeks God" (Rom. 3:11). The reconciliation of these two statements, that people "should seek God" and that "no one seeks God" is best made by thinking that we who retain the image of God even in our sin, whose hearts are indeed restless until they find their rest in God their Creator, find ourselves always frustrated in this search outside of Christ. We both need him and yet do not want him. We need God, but we will not accept him except on our own terms—unless God's grace intervenes! These are the contradictions that rattle through the being of every sinner!

And this is really the way in which the nature of sin, as it were, exposes itself. It is as if someone were determined to embarrass him or herself by stripping in public. After all, how did this internal, misunderstood yearning for something larger than itself come to expression? The answer, of course, is in crass idolatry! We "ought not to think that the divine being is like gold or silver or stone, an image formed by the art and imagination of man" (Acts 17:29). Idol makers inevitably set themselves up as being somewhat on a par with the idols they have made, and postmoderns likewise think that God can be had on their terms as consumers. They think God can be accessed internally, when it is convenient, on the consumer's own terms. In so doing, they are making a mistake that is as foolish and as crass as the Athenian idolaters were making. God forbore in the past but no longer (17:30). The command has gone out to repent (17:30).

By this stage in his address, Paul had already set up his doctrine of human nature and now goes on to add that of salvation. On the former, contrary to pagan notions and, for that matter, modern notions, there have not been multiple origins to the human race. Then, they thought that every ethnic group had its own original starting point, and today many think that the human race had several spontaneous originations along the evolutionary way. Not so! He "made from one man every nation of mankind to live on the face of the earth" (17:26). There was a single origination, and though Adam and Eve are not mentioned, this clearly was what Paul had in mind. Nor does Luke record whether Paul then set up a parallel, as he was to do in Romans, between "one man" through whom sin has come and the "one man Jesus Christ" from whom we receive grace and righteousness (Rom. 5:12, 15). Yet this is clearly the direction in which Paul's mind moved.

What Luke does record for us is that Paul spoke of this salvation in two related connections. First, it is by this Christ that divine judgment will be discharged in this world and, second, the evidence that this is the case lies in his resurrection (Acts 17:31). What else Paul said on that day we are not told, because it was the resurrection that immediately provoked such scorn among some of the listeners and brought this address to an abrupt end (17:32). Yet here are lines in Pauline thought with which we are quite familiar. It was the resurrection that showed Christ to be the Son of God and Lord (Rom. 1:3–4). The connection between resurrection and salvation is stated directly in another Romans passage where Paul says "if you confess with your mouth that Jesus is Lord and believe in your heart that God raised him from the dead, you will be saved" (Rom. 10:9). Without this resurrection, Christian witness is fraudulent, preaching is empty, sins are unforgiven, and all hope is lost (1 Cor. 15:14–15, 18). Perhaps the conceptual connections between these ideas—how the cross is related to divine judgment on the one side and to Christ's resurrection on the other—were spelled out on that day, though in his brief summary Luke makes no mention of this. Yet we do know that for Paul there could be no gospel without Christ's cross, no cross without a resurrection, and no resurrection without salvation and judgment.

A Model Engagement

Changed as our world may be, Paul's missionary address to the pagans in Athens on this occasion is as current as it was on the day in which he delivered it. More than that, it is a model for how we should be engaging our own postmodern world in the West. Some evangelicals have tried to see in Luke's account an example of how Paul was able to exploit the culture for the sake of the gospel. What they mean is that he was able to capitalize on their cultural habits to "sell" the gospel. They could not be more wrong! What we see is Paul confronting his culture, not trying to use it, and this is evident from the fact that he starts, not with the gospel itself but with that culture's competing worldviews, each one of which he demolishes. It was only after this work of demolition was completed that Paul then turned to the gospel, and that only happened at the very end of his address. In the example that we have of Paul's pioneering engagement with pagan culture, two main ideas stand out.

First, Paul declared the unique truth claims of Christ and rejected every other truth claim. He passed up every opportunity that his setting offered him to suggest that Christ was not the exclusive way to God. No doubt, had he conceded that there are many ways to God, his audience would have been rather pleased because the exclusivity of Christian claims was an aggravation to them. Certainly, they found his message "strange" (Acts 17:20) because they found the idea of the resurrection of Christ strange. Paul, however, refused to go down the path of religious pluralism.

Early in his address, Paul cited the reality of natural revelation, the fact that people have within them an awareness of the sacred or divine. This sense found expression then in the rampant forms of pagan worship that Paul had witnessed in the city. It is finding expression today in the West in the rampant forms of spirituality that we see on every side. It would have been so simple then to say, as many evangelicals are finding it convenient to say now, that pagans had started down the right road but had not traveled far enough, that they had come a long way toward finding Jesus, and that all they had to do was just to take a few more steps.

The truth of the matter, however, is that natural revelation does not provide us with the building blocks from which we can assemble a knowledge of God that is saving. The saving knowledge of God is not assembled by us but given by God. It is not harvested from the fragments of our experience in this world but created *de novo* by the sovereign working of God. It is a knowledge that comes from *above* in conjunction with the person of Christ and his grace; it does not come from *below* in our strivings to make spiritual connections with the larger Whole. We contribute nothing to our salvation except the sin from which we need to be redeemed, as William Temple said, and we are accepted by God through Christ only on his terms and not on our terms at all.

Secondly, Paul's apologetic would have fallen flat on its face had he not been so knowledgeable of the world in which he lived. He was conversant with his culture. He had a detailed knowledge of its philosophies and religions. He apparently knew them like the back of his hand. That was why, when this unexpected invitation came to speak to the intellectuals assembled at Mars Hill, he could avail himself of it on the spot. He was clearly at home in this kind of world, and he showed how the people in this sort of setting could be engaged without the Christian gospel being compromised.

Paul's assumption on this occasion was quite different from what passes in much of the evangelical world today, at least in the West. Paul assumed that his culture was fallen, its religions mistaken, and that redemption meant a clean break with all "natural" religion. We tend to assume the opposite. We read Barna polls assiduously to find the best ways to capitalize on the culture, to find the stars to which the gospel wagon can be hitched. Evangelicals in their droves are rushing to embrace what they think is "culture" (though what they are really talking about is mostly passing fads and fashions) in the forlorn hope that they will find in it the recipe for their own success and acceptance. Paul, on this occasion, was driven by a contrary mind, in fact by a clear sense of antithesis to much of what he saw. He did not do what so many evangelicals are doing, which is seeking to identify with what is culturally *au courant*, with the latest, what is most *in* so as to win some supposed acceptance in the postmodern world. Here is the old liberal "Christ-of-culture" position. What a pathetic spectacle it is! Surely the angels must be averting their eyes as today's Christian media revels in reporting all that is happening as if it were normative and, indeed, admirable!

What results from this kind of accommodation to the culture is that the Christian gospel comes to seem little different from the kind of general spirituality that is now pervasive throughout all Western cultures. For a long time, in fact, evangelicals have been in the business of minimizing and reducing the gospel to its bare essentials, putting it in the most appealing secular form, selling and marketing it, and stripping it of its doctrinal framework. Any kind of doctrine present in the framing of the gospel, it is believed, will put people off, and so, to assure more success, all doctrine has now gone. The gospel is reduced to purely relational terms: sin is only what prevents us from reaching our full potential; God is anxiously yearning for a relationship with us, which he has been unable to bring about because he has not been able to catch our attention; for a one-time admission of weakness, people can receive the eternal benefits of having God on their side. It is all so easy! Why would anyone even hesitate to clinch such an advantageous deal?

What is rapidly filling evangelical churches, however, is not the kind of spirituality that is the fruit of the gospel but, rather, the kind of spirituality that can be had without Christ at all. The kind of spirituality that is being offered—a spirituality without doctrinal truth, without the full recognition of the reality of sin, without any sense of the due holiness of God, and without too much need for the cross—is little different from the spirituality pervasive in the culture, a spirituality which is often not religious. The gospel being marketed to postmodern consumers is a gospel perverted by these same postmodern consumers who have been encouraged to think that they can "buy" on their own terms. And those terms have far more in common with paganism than we realize or might like to know!

The issue, then as now, is whether we can approach God on our own terms, take him as we want, and use him as we will, or not. Pagans then were not like the children of the Enlightenment: rationalistic, naturalistic, and reductionistic. No, they were spiritual people, but people whose spirituality was sought as an insurance policy against the hazards of life. The hazards they feared were very different from the hazards we fear. They feared the dark forces outside themselves, the forces of the gods and goddesses. We fear the dark forces within us. We are therefore on the hunt for insurance policies against ourselves, against our own boredom, emptiness, anxiety, and sense of being adrift in an ocean so vast as to make its far shores invisible. This is where people today have their vulnerabilities. And this is precisely where the church is mostly pitching its message: to those who live a privatized existence, haunted by their own emptiness, and hungry for therapeutic relief. And biblical truth, apparently, has little to do with that!

The problem with this approach is that the gospel today has become little different from any of the other therapies and self-help regimes that are on the market. This is precisely what Paul resisted when it was open for him to say that the gospel was, in fact, just another form of the kind of religion that was already present in Athens. He refused to walk down that road, as we ourselves should.

The gospel we preach will be different from the "gospel" of our current, postmodern spirituality only when we learn to do what the apostle Paul did in Athens. He analyzed and critiqued the worldviews of his day within which paganism was nestled. We do not. He worked hard at this. We do not. He did this because his spirituality was up to the task. Ours often is not. This is work that requires tough intellectual slogging. It requires stringent moral judgments. This is no superficial activity but one which should spring from the depths of our being. And what it will yield will not be quick and easy results. There is the possibility, though, if we will but pay the price, that a foundation will be laid for authentic Christian believing. Why, one wonders, would we want anything else?

2

One God

PETER R. JONES

In the beginning God created the heavens and the earth.

GENESIS 1:1[1]

In 1974 Christian America witnessed the publication of David Miller's *The New Polytheism*. The author, professor of religion at Syracuse University and for many years a member of the publication board of the Society of Biblical Literature, belonged to the group of scholars known as the "death of God" theologians. When I arrived in the United States from Britain in 1964, I was asked to read these theologians. At the time we rested assured that the "death of God" was the passing fad of a few marginal radical scholars. But Miller thought differently. *The New Polytheism* announced with great foresight and unabashed glee the funeral of the God of the Bible and triumphantly heralded the rebirth of the gods and goddesses of ancient Greece and Rome:

> The announcement of the death of God was the obituary of a useless single-minded and one-dimensional norm of a civilization that has been predominantly monotheistic, not only in its reli-

---

[1] Unless otherwise noted, Scripture references quoted in this chapter are taken from the *New International Version* of the Bible (NIV).

gion, but also in its politics, its history, its social order, its ethics, and its psychology. When released from the tyrannical imperialism of monotheism by the death of God, man has the opportunity of discovering new dimensions hidden in the depths of reality's history.[2]

Miller was not alone. In 1997 Jean Houston said: "Now open your eyes and look at all the gods in hiding,"[3] waiting, she clearly meant, now to be rediscovered.

Many Christians will receive such news as harmless babble from the radical fringe. But ideas have consequences. One generation after the publication of the *New Polytheism*, we saw the publication of *The Omni-gendered Society* by Virginia Ramey Mollenkott, which describes the unraveling of single-minded, monotheistic thinking in our society. We now have two kinds of marriage—straight and gay—and acceptance of a third arrangement—polygamy—cannot be far behind. Polytheism immediately gives us polysexuality. In similar ways, polytheistic thinking is extending its influence in every category of human life.

The Pagan, Polytheistic Challenge

Western polytheism is maturing. One recent book was titled *The Deities Are Many: A Polytheistic Theology*.[4] The author was a Western scholar raised in a Jewish home on the credo: "Hear O Israel, the LORD your God, the LORD is one." Through an initial attraction to Buddhism, he finally ended up in North American Indian shamanism. The book is purported to be the first systematic apologetic for polytheistic theology, claiming that polytheism is inherent in human nature, and that monotheism is extremely recent,

---

[2] David LeRoy Miller, *The New Polytheism* (New York: Harper & Row, 1974), vii.

[3] Jean Houston, *A Passion for the Possible: A Guide to Realizing Your True Potential* (San Francisco: HarperSanFrancisco, 1997), 20, cited in Herrick, *The Making,* 177.

[4] Jordan D. Paper, *The Deities Are Many: A Polytheistic Theology* (Albany, NY: State University of New York Press, 2005).

arose in a tiny part of the planet, and is constantly breaking down. The author admits that his primary understanding of the deities comes not from study but from direct experience with them. Mystical occult experience is the real source of polytheistic theology.

Many Christians will be surprised to learn that the chief doctrinal attack in our time is directed not to the inspiration of Scripture or the deity of Christ, but to the doctrine of God. The very denial of God is one of the chief obstacles to our preaching of the gospel today. Camille Paglia, provocative lesbian philosopher, begins her book *Sexual Personae* with these words: "In the beginning was Nature."[5] Robert Mueller, former assistant general secretary of the United Nations, said: "There is no 'In the beginning, God created . . .' at the UN." For many in our day, biblical theism is no longer the starting point of their thinking.

Let me provide some striking examples of this doctrinal assault against the one God. Jean Houston, the counselor of Hillary Clinton, has written that our present society is in a state of both "breakdown and breakthrough . . . what I call a whole system transition . . . requir[ing] a new alignment that only myth can bring."[6] This appears in her book *The Passion of Isis and Osiris*.

On September 8, 2000, President Bill Clinton held a reception for an incredible assembly of world leaders made up of dignitaries, ambassadors, and heads of state who were attending the United Nations Millennium Summit. The reception was held in one of the most remarkable places in New York City: the Temple of Dendur, a Nubian shrine honoring the Egyptian goddess Isis. The temple was rebuilt stone by stone in the Sackler Wing of the Metropolitan Museum of Art, a large glass room overlooking Central Park.

The 2000 Millennium Summit established The United Nations

---

[5] Camille Paglia, *Sexual Personae: Art & Decadence from Nefertiti to Emily Dickinson* (New Haven, CT: Yale University Press, 1990).
[6] Jean Houston, *The Passion of Isis and Osiris: A Gateway to Transcendent Love* (New York: Ballantine, 1995), 2.

Development Program (UNDP), now in 166 countries, of which Houston is a senior consultant. UNDP sponsors Houston's work in leadership training, "directing both individual and social capital toward the creation of better societies and peoples . . . providing strategies that can work in an interconnected world."[7] What strategies does Houston use? Going to all the undeveloped countries of the world and supported by United States tax dollars, she trains young leaders in "social artistry," reconnecting them with their old pagan ancestral myths. It is only the mythologically wise community that refocuses society to deeper maturity, she says. This, if the United Nations has anything to do with it, will be the basis of the planetary community. At the foundation of the new world civilization will be a totally different view of God from that taught in the Bible.

A Wiccan group on the West Coast, Reclaiming, proposes a "community of women and men working to unify spirit and politics. Our vision is rooted in the religion and magic of the Goddess—the Immanent Life Force. . . . We use the skills we learn to . . . bring to birth a vision of a new culture." Such ideas are even more widespread in Europe than in America. In Great Britain only 23 [percent] believe in a personal God; 44 [percent] in "some sort of spirit or life force." In Sweden 15 [percent] believe in a personal God; 44 [percent] in a spirit force.[8]

These trends signify a genuine threat to the world that is presently emerging. These ideas are like noxious gases escaping from the first small crack in the earth's crust before a major volcano breaks open a massive fault line, and burning lava consumes all around it. In the appearance of this marginal alternate spirituality we are witnessing the first signs of a major religious revolution that threatens to sweep all before it.

Like a volcanic mountain before its eruption, our world is

---

[7] http://www.undp.org.
[8] Hugh McCloed and Werner Ulstorf, *The Decline of Christendom in Western Europe, 1750–2000* (Cambridge: Cambridge University Press, 2003), 48.

experiencing underground pressures that pose an opportunity for polytheistic spirituality. Religious paganism offers an exit strategy from the impasse of the postmodern and the confusion of deconstruction. And while Christians are busy placing their fingers in the postmodern dike of our civilization the intellectual neo-pagans are producing a worldview as composite and coherent as any on offer. They offer the following:

- a powerful experience of spirituality, a discovery of the subconscious which provides an exit from the failure of rationalism;
- a solution to the conflict between science and religion;
- a critique of Western philosophy—with its rationalism, materialism, and consumerism—as sharp and compelling as that of the best Christian accounts;
- an enchanted, passionate, and environmentally informed view of nature;
- an end to religious strife;
- an all-encompassing geopolitical vision of planetary harmony;
- a spirituality that is palatable to the toleration demands of the public square;
- an all-inclusive, cradle-to-grave, spiritually inspired educational policy;
- a powerfully therapeutic psychology that delivers from anger and greed and proposes an experience of rebirth;
- a radical liberation of narrow heterosexuality into the pleasure-filled paths of pansexuality; and
- an evolutionary account of history and of human significance.

This is the polytheistic armada breaking upon the shores of the land once known as Christendom—all attractively presented in an intellectually satisfying, well-planned, and coherent package. Amazingly, this agenda is proposed to our relativized, deconstructed world, as "timeless . . . perennial . . . truth"[9] with exuberant, infinite possibilities.[10] This is the emerging challenge to our

---

[9] Smith, 58.
[10] Ibid., 60–61.

biblical worldview, and Christians will need to be up to the demands of this coherent agenda. The "new" culture of tomorrow's world—the world of our children and grandchildren—will be a spiritual world, but one not based on the Bible's view of God. If this comes to pass, the Christian church may face its gravest threat since the Roman Empire.

Why should Christians consider neo-paganism such a threat? Contemporary sociologists speak of "the subjective turn" of modern culture: a turning away from life as "established roles" and "given orders of things" to states of consciousness, bodily experiences, and the occult life of the unconscious as the norms of behavior. Such a turn fits with the passage from the modern rational structures to the postmodern deconstruction of life and language. This turn can also be described as a turn from objective religion to subjective spirituality—that is, from religion as giving norms of transcendent meaning to spirituality that celebrates subjective experience. Because it fits with the broader subjective turn of postmodernity, this spirituality, say the sociologists, is on the rise. Some describe this religious change as "a tectonic shift on the sacred landscape that will prove even more significant than the Protestant Reformation."[11]

In his book, *The Death of Christian Britain*, church historian Callum Brown states, "Britain is showing the world how religion as we know it can die."[12] The churchman Peter Brierley says, "We are one generation from extinction."[13] The demise of Christianity and the rise of pagan spirituality in Great Britain is called a "major spiritual revolution."[14]

But did we not already write off godless Europe? These British

---

[11] Paul Heelas and Linda Woodhead, *The Spiritual Revolution: Why Religion Is Giving Way to Spirituality* (Oxford: Blackwell, 2005), 2.

[12] Callum Brown, *The Death of Christian Britain* (London: Routledge, 2001), 198.

[13] Peter Brierley, *Religious Trends* (London: Marshall Pickering, 1999).

[14] See the title of the book by Paul Heelas and Linda Woodhead, *The Spiritual Revolution: Why Religion Is Giving Way to Spirituality* (Oxford: Blackwell, 2005).

sociologists make a passing remark that should get our attention: "It could be the case that there is more evidence for the spiritual revolution claim in the USA than in Britain."[15] They give as evidence the trend in church attendance in the United States, which has fallen from 40 percent in the 1960s to 22 to 24 percent today; the 15,000 sites advertising yoga programs in New York; the 15 million yoga practitioners as of 2002, and the 35.3 million Americans who said in 2003 that they intended to take up yoga in the future. In 2005, 35 million were practicing yoga, including many Christians.

The growth of non-Christian spirituality poses Christians with both a challenge and an opportunity. The polytheistic neo-pagan moment in contemporary Western history provides a unique God-ordained occasion for full-orbed, biblical witness. It is the moment for Christians:

- to reengage the culture at the level of worldview—this is a new day for Reformed, presuppositional apologetics in a postmodern world;
- to seize the occasion of religious clarity that the face-off between monism and theism allows, and thus break down the grey confusion of politically-correct postmodern pluralism;
- to understand thoroughly the worldview of paganism to better engage the contemporary seeker of truth;
- to render the pagan worldview coherent for the laity and for our rising generation of students in order that they be equipped for witness to a pagan world and have the courage to speak up and speak out intelligently in the mind-numbing but intimidating world of politically correct newspeak;
- to seize the occasion, as people begin to see through the pagan lie and are disillusioned with a paganized, half-hearted form of Christianity, to bring a fully-informed restatement of biblical theism and of Reformed theology—the only real answer to the pagan challenge.

---

[15] Bob Smietana, "Statistical Illusion: New study confirms that we go to church much less than we say," *Christianity Today* (April, 2006).

There are two views of God in deep conflict today—as they were in the ancient world—two meta-narratives in radical opposition to one another, and the struggle has only just begun.

In facing the threat and embracing the challenge before us today, the first step is to understand the challenge rightly. The battleground of today and tomorrow is over the doctrine of God himself. To the pagan, everything is divine and the cosmos is God. God is the predicate, not the subject. Hence, "*love* is God": we creatures confer divinity on elements within the cosmos. But in the Bible we find the precise opposite. God is the originating subject before whom we bow in wonder and praise, whereas the creation is predicate. *God* is love. Only God the Creator is divine: everything else in the cosmos is created by and for him.

The Biblical Witness to the One True God

When we think of God as the great, transcendent subject of all reality, we are naturally reminded of the stunning statement of theology and cosmology that begins the Bible: "In the beginning, God created the heavens and the earth" (Gen. 1:1).

The Bible does not begin: *In the beginning was spiritual experience*, or even, *In the beginning, Christ died for our sins*. However much we may glory in that truth, this is not where the Word of God begins. It begins with a majestic statement about the objective, transcendent character of God the Creator. In other words, it begins with a statement of cosmology and theology, not with a declaration of soteriology or pneumatology. The first verse of the Bible is a resounding, alien, programmatic declaration of biblical theism that throws down the gauntlet before the second millennium BC world of all-embracing Egyptian and Canaanite pagan monism. In our day of revived paganism, this same declaration needs to be heard with force once again if there is to be a revival of true faith.

Genesis 1:1 reveals an objective God who is separate from the cosmos. This was the point of Francis Schaeffer's early book, *The*

God Who Is There.[16] This title is like the phrase, "everywhere you go, there you are." If this phrase applies to anyone, it surely applies first and foremost to God, so why bother saying it? It became meaningful to me when I read the work of a modern pagan, Joseph Campbell, guru to George Lucas of *Star Wars* fame. Campbell wrote: "In religions where the god or creator is the mother, the world is her body. *There is nowhere else*" [emphasis added].[17] There is no *there*. In such a view, God has no place or existence of his own. The creation is God, and apart from the trees and rivers and mountains, God possesses no *there*. But, as Schaeffer pointed out, Genesis 1:1 declares that God is there. Apart from and before the creation, there is God! God is not defined by the creation, but creation and all creatures are defined by *the God who is there*.

The Christian worldview—focused on the Bible, which begins, "In the beginning, God . . ."—declares the one true God who is there. Genesis 1:1 makes a number of points that uphold the Christian worldview and witness against the pagan, polytheistic challenge. What are they? Genesis 1:1 declares that God is the eternal Creator, who is unique, transcendent, personal, sovereign, and holy.

Eternal. The beginning is the beginning of the cosmos, not of God, the beginning of God's work of creation. God is not the first in a series, from which everything else emanates in a chain of divine being. God has no beginning. Thus creation is *ex nihilo*. There is majestic mystery here. As Ecclesiastes tells us: "He has made everything beautiful in its time. Also, he has put eternity into man's heart, yet so that he cannot find out what God has done from the beginning to the end" (3:11). The prophet Habakkuk marveled, "Are you not from everlasting, O LORD my God, my

---

[16] Francis Schaeffer, *The God Who Is There: Speaking Historic Christianity into the Twentieth Century* (Chicago: InterVarsity, 1968).
[17] Joseph Campbell and Bill Moyers, *The Power of Myth* (New York: Anchor Books/Doubleday, 1988), 58.

Holy One?" (Hab. 1:12). Here is the great biblical distinction between the Creator and creation that stands at the heart of the religion of the Bible.

Because God is the Alpha and Omega, there is an absolute beginning to the cosmos and an absolute ending, and thus we can speak of genuine history—what neopaganism rejects in classic postmodern language as "the absolute displacement of mythic cyclism by egoic linearity."[18] But history exists because God is before it and after it; God is eternal.

Creator. God is eternal because he is Creator. God asks: "'To whom will you compare me? Or who is my equal?' says the Holy One. 'Lift your eyes and look to the heavens: Who created all these?'" (Isa. 40:25–26). Christians do not believe that God *is* the creation or a sort of impersonal spirit within all things. While the imprint of his creative hand is truly on everything (Rom. 1:19–20), God is nevertheless different from what he has made, just as a watchmaker is not a watch.

Critical scholars sometimes admit that the Christian message is unique in this claim. Far from being one ancient myth among many, the Bible lays out a message not found in any other ancient text. The Bible is different, and brings a unique message. Klaus Westermann, the critical German Old Testament scholar, explains: "What distinguishes the [Genesis] account of creation among the many creation stories of the Ancient Near East is that for Genesis there can be only one creator and that all else that is or can be, can never be anything but a creature."[19]

Unique. This is a unique message, to be found only in the Bible. It follows that God is unique. God the Eternal Creator is also unique. Because God is the Creator, the Bible insists on his uniqueness. Note

---

[18] Sean Kelly, *Individuation and the Absolute: Hegel, Jung, and the Path Toward Wholeness* (New York: Paulist Press, 1993), website chapter (http://www.ciis.edu).

[19] Klaus Westermann, *Genesis 1–11: A Commentary*, trans. J. J. Scullion (Minneapolis: Augsburg Press, 1984), 127.

again God's affirmation through Isaiah, "'To whom will you compare me? Or who is my equal?' says the Holy One" (Isa. 40:25).

A pantheon of deities did not produce the marvel of creation. A humorous adage asks, "What is a camel?" and answers, "A horse designed by committee!" But that is not what creation actually reveals. There is a great mind at work creating mind-boggling diversity. D. A. Carson remarks, "God creates snowflakes; we produce ice-cubes."[20] There is no equal to God. This is why it is such an affront to make images of God.[21] Nothing in the created order is like him. Idols don't show people to be primitive savages so much as they prove them to be sophisticated worshipers of nature as divine. God is jealous, not because he is insecure, but because he insists that the true nature of things and of himself be known.

"Hear, O Israel, the LORD our GOD, the LORD is one" (Deut. 6:4) is the historic credo of Israel in the ancient polytheistic world. Especially in the struggle against eighth-century all-powerful Babylonian paganism, God constantly insisted through Isaiah that there can be no idols because he is incomparable, and he is incomparable because he is unique: "I am the LORD, and there is no other" (Isa. 45:6; 46:9). See how the gnostics later in church history mocked at God, calling him "the Blind One" for saying this, because there clearly is another, the Great Spirit. Against that same mockery we must declare the name of the one unique God in our time. Genesis 1:1 declares monotheism, not polytheism; one God, not many; not one God and many little ones.

Transcendent. The Creator is unique but also transcendent. Polytheistic gods are not transcendent; neither is the one divine spirit of classic paganism both ancient and modern. Neither is the God of Episcopal bishop John Shelby Spong transcendent. Speaking in a televised interview, he revealed: "When I define

---

[20] D. A. Carson, *The Gagging of God: Christianity Confronts Pluralism* (Grand Rapids, MI: Zondervan, 1996), 97.
[21] Exodus 20:4–5.

God . . . it's not as a being upstairs . . . I experience God . . . as the power of life. I experience God as the power of love. I experience God in the words of my favorite theologian, Paul Tillich, as the ground of being."[22]

In contrast, since the Bible describes God the Creator as unique—unlike anything else—we call him *transcendent*, or *other*, because he goes infinitely beyond anything else we know. This is the kind of God we need—a real God and not a human clone.

J. Gresham Machen, a stalwart defender of Christian orthodoxy writing in the 1920s, saw the beginning of the radical apostate movement. Machen saw liberalism entering the mainline churches as paganism in Christian dress,[23] and he adeptly put his finger on the essence of this apostasy at a time when it was not so obvious:

> The truth is that liberalism has lost sight of the very center and core of the Christian teaching . . . one attribute of God is absolutely fundamental in the Bible . . . in order to render intelligible all the rest. *That attribute is the awful transcendence of God.* It is true, indeed, that not a sparrow falls to the ground without him. But he is immanent in the world not because he is identified with the world, but because he is the free Creator and upholder of it. Between the creature and the Creator a great gulf is fixed [emphasis added].[24]

From the truth about God's transcendence flows what theologians call God's incommunicable attributes. This does not mean that God is not good at communicating. He created communication. It means there are some things in his divine nature he cannot share with us because he is transcendent in his being. Here is a sample list:

---

[22] John Shelby Spong, interviewed on Fox News, April 13, 2005.

[23] Machen used the synonym *naturalism* for what I refer to as *paganism*.

[24] J. Gresham Machen, *Christianity and Liberalism* (Grand Rapids, MI: Eerdmans, 1923), 62–63.

- God had no beginning, creation did;
- God is independent, we are dependent;
- God has the attribute of eternity, we have a beginning;
- God is immutable, we are changing;
- God is infinite, we are finite;
- God is all-powerful (*omnipotent*), we clearly are not;
- God is all-knowing (*omniscient*), our knowledge is limited;
- God knows things before they happen, we do not;
- God's presence is felt in every nook and cranny of the cosmos (*omnipresent*), we are limited in space and time;[25]
- God is absolute, we are relative;
- God is perfect being, we are derivative beings.

Since none of these attributes can ever be said about creatures, do not let anyone tell you that you can become God. The only way that can happen is to change your idea of God, and that god is no god at all. That is man trying to be God—which is the essence of pagan idolatry!

Personal and triune. God the unique, transcendent Creator is also personal and truine. How could such a formidable God be also personal? Wouldn't you be scared of a God like that? Well, yes, like Aslan, in C. S. Lewis's Narnia books. Aslan was awesome and fearsome, though completely good. He also was a person—he could be known and loved personally, just as he was a person who knew and loved. But not so the pagan divine. June Singer, the Jungian psychologist, was raised as a Jew before converting to Gnosticism. But her writing shows a total ignorance for the God of her fathers when she says: "The creator god is in a state of "utter Loneliness . . . in the midst of endless emptiness."[26]

The biblical doctrine of the Trinity reveals that God is not only personal, but *transcendently* personal. That is, he does not need you or me to get close and personal. The Gospel of John begins,

---

[25] Even New Age, occultic astral travel does not come close to divine omnipresence.

[26] June Singer, *Androgyny: Towards a New Theory of Sexuality* (London: Routledge and Kegan, 1977), 61.

like Genesis, by describing divine creation. But John adds more clarity to the plural name *Elohim*: "In the beginning was the Word, and the Word was with God, and the Word was God . . . through [the Word] all things were made" (John 1:1–3). The God behind the created world is "a self-contained union of three divine persons, Father, Son and Spirit, a communion of persons existing in loving relations . . . who does not need the world."[27] In the Trinity there is quite enough love and personal communion to go around forever. This is also why the Bible maintains the Creator/creature distinction—because in the Trinity God has his own sphere of existence. God is not some lone, eternal spirit, forever contemplating himself and longing to create human companions. God was not cosmically lonely in need of human friends or personal affirmation. He only creates out of love for the creature, and for his own glory.

But Paganism renders God diffuse. In Neale Donald Walsch's *Conversations with God for Teens*, "God" says to Luciano, a young inquirer from Italy: "When it no longer serves you to know yourself as Luciano, you will meld into The Oneness and be the part of me that has no individual identity."[28] No one quite knows where they are or even whether they exist. Thus the one circle of pagan unity turns out to be a foreboding black hole of impersonal nothingness. Some would call that hell.

The Bible proposes a personal relationship with the Maker of heaven and earth. That relationship is already seen in the Old Testament, but comes to its pinnacle in Jesus Christ and in his gift of the Holy Spirit. God's presence is intimate, comforting, and real. Creatures can know the joy of deep personal intimacy with their Maker.

Christians pray; pagans meditate. Christian prayer uses words;

---

[27] Colin E. Gunton, *The Triune Creator: A Historical and Systematic Study* (Grand Rapids, MI: Eerdmans, 1998), 9.

[28] Neale Donald Walsch's *Conversations with God for Teens* (Scholastic, New York: 2001), 314–15.

pagan mediation kills the mind. In prayer Christians praise the Creator; in mediation one observes and lauds oneself. We can lose ourselves, that is, our harmful preoccupation with ourselves, in genuine acts of adoration for the God outside. We address the personal Creator who truly is *there*. And the personal God answers the door when we knock.[29]

Once you admit this biblical understanding of God, Christianity makes a lot of sense. Theism is not the faith of bigoted people who refuse to fit in or get along. It is the truth about who we are as finite people in an amazing, beautifully designed universe that we did not make, face to face with the personal God who did. Why am I a theist? It is why Job was a theist. Because only God could be the author of the event that radically determines my entire existence, past, present and future, over which I have absolutely no control—namely, my creation. I do not—I cannot—claim this power.[30] I merely recognize and praise the transcendent power and amazing love of another.

Sovereign. God the unique, transcendent, personal Creator is also sovereign. By his free choice God is the sovereign, unique Creator of the cosmos. Like Job we must cry out, "I know that you can do all things; no plan of yours can be thwarted" (Job 42:2). And like the psalmist, "Our God is in heaven; he does whatever pleases him" (Ps. 115:3). God's sovereignty is compared to the weakness of the pagan idols: "Bel bows down, Nebo stoops low; their idols are borne by beasts of burden; the images that are carried about are burdensome, a burden for the weary" (Isa. 46:1). Isaiah therefore warns the people that while they have to carry the idols, all their lives God has been carrying them. If they will turn from the idols and return to the Lord, they will not find him a burden: "Even to your old age I am he, and to gray hairs I will carry

---

[29] Revelation 3:20 cf. Matthew 7:7: "Ask and it will be given to you; seek and you will find; knock and the door will be opened to you."
[30] Job 40:3–42:6.

you. I have made you and I will carry you; I will sustain you and I will rescue you" (Isa. 46:4). The reason for this is the sovereignty of God. Isaiah explains: "I am God, and there is no other; I am God, and there is none like me. I make known the end from the beginning†and from ancient times things not yet done, saying, 'My counsel shall stand, and I will accomplish all my purpose'" (Isa. 46:9–10).

God in his essence is sovereign, so he is sovereign both in nature and in grace. Therefore, Paul asks us:

> Who are you, O man, to talk back to God? Shall what is formed say to him who formed it, "Why did you make me like this?" Does not the potter have the right to make out of the same lump of clay some pottery for noble purposes and some for common use? (Rom. 9:20–21)

In placing creatures on the same level with the unique Creator, we make for ourselves great logical problems between divine sovereignty and human responsibility. To be sure, there is great mystery here, but once you understand the biblical revelation of the one unique God, the very fact of this mystery makes sense.

The biblical Calvinist has had a Job-like experience. Before the reality of God, Job finally learned the only possible answers: "I am unworthy—how can I reply to you? I put my hand over my mouth. . . . I know that you can do all things; no plan of yours can be thwarted" (Job 40:4; 42:2). Yet those who know God can say with Abraham: "Shall not the Judge of all the earth do right?" (Gen. 18:25 KJV).

Holy. God the eternal, unique, transcendent, personal and sovereign Creator is also *holy.* God as One is an essential element of biblical holiness. Because God is the unique Creator, separate from the creation, he is holy. When someone uses the word *holy,* many in the world think of people like Mother Teresa, people with apparently pure lives and an impeccable public record of self-giving.

But to say "God is there" is to affirm his holiness. To give God a distinct *place* is to sanctify him, because the root meaning of *holy* is "set apart." God cannot be confused with the powers of nature that the pagans make into divine beings. Everything, even God, has its special place. For instance, no one was to enter the temple of the Lord except the priests and Levites on duty: "they may enter because they are consecrated [made holy, that is, set apart], but all the other men are to guard what the LORD has assigned to them" (2 Chron. 23:6). These priests were holy, not because of unusual moral purity, but because God had set them apart for a special, priestly task. Even their robes were holy, because the robes had been "set apart" (see Ex. 28:4).

The command to acknowledge God as holy means to set him apart as unique, that is, not to confuse him with other claimants to deity. Nor is it to confuse him with what he has made. "This is what the LORD says: 'Heaven is my throne, and the earth is my footstool'" (Isa. 66:1; cf. Matt. 5:35; Acts 7:49). Granting him that special high location of his own throne, rather than confusing him with the earthly footstool, makes God holy in our eyes, honors him in his unique place, and recognizes his unique being.

In one of his well-known prayers, the Lord's Prayer, Jesus teaches us that we are to pray, "Hallowed [holy] be your name" (Matt. 6:9). Sure, we make God's name holy by not misusing it (see Ex. 20:7). If we apply God's holy name to something or someone who is not God, we profane that name. We are not to pray like the pagans who, with their mantras, do not address the true, personal God, and whose view of God as the force within nature does not hallow his name.

We also fail to hallow God's name when we claim, in mysticism, to share in God's divine substance. Meister Eckhart, the so-called Christian mystic, claimed "something in the soul that is uncreated and uncreatable."[31] But this is not true. It is no more *Christian* than the statement of Yale Professor Harold Bloom, a Jew who became a gnostic, who said somewhere, "I am uncreated, as old as God." The truth is we will always be creatures. This is our calling and glory. To step over this line is idolatry. If holiness is first and foremost things and persons in their rightful places, then God's place as separate from creation—the biblical doctrine of God—is the fundamental starting point for *our* notions of holiness. Therefore the pagan denial of theism—even as it uses words like god and divinity—is fundamentally unholy, and so then are the spirituality and life-choices made on this unholy *spiritual* basis.

The glory of God is his holiness—that is, his divine otherness that goes beyond anything we creatures could ever imagine. A man who survived the tsunami in Sri Lanka said it was like being tossed about in a great washing machine. A true encounter with God is like that; his holiness literally blows us away. One who came close to God, Isaiah, was sure that his days were up. "Woe is me!" he cried. "For I am lost" (Isa. 6:5 ESV).

This great and courageous eighth-century prophet, who like few others understood and took on the power of the surrounding Babylonian paganism, also understood the Creator/creature distinction. In 739 BC when King Uzziah died,[32] Isaiah saw the glory of the Lord and heard angelic voices. Their sound, he said, shook the doorposts and threshold of the temple, as they cried to one another: "Holy, holy, holy is the LORD Almighty; the whole earth is full of his glory" (Isa. 6:3).

This majestic *Sanctus of the Seraphim* takes up the great declaration of Psalm 8: "O LORD, our Lord, how majestic is your name in all the earth!" (v. 1). The Seraphim declare both the holiness of

---

[31] Cited by Huston Smith, 62.
[32] According to J. N. Oswalt, *The Book of Isaiah: Chapters 1–39* (Grand Rapids, MI: Eerdmans, 1986), 176.

God, and by extension and reflection in its God-designed complexity, the holiness of his created handiwork. To this we are called to witness in our speech and in our own lives of holiness.

This is the God to whom we bear witness in a more and more religiously pagan world that no longer wants to hear of such a God nor see the reality of holy living by those who worship him. But on this there can be no compromise. We must confess with boldness and humility, with the prophets and apostles of old: "To the King eternal, immortal, invisible, the only God, be honor and glory forever and ever. Amen" (1 Tim. 1:17).

At the Beginning and End: God

The lines are drawn. This is where the battle is engaged in our day. The conflict is not about details, nor is the disagreement of recent date. About this the Bible has something to say. Three thousand years ago the psalmist sang: "I said to the LORD, 'You are my Lord; apart from you I have no good thing.' As for the pagan priests who are in the land, and the nobles in whom all delight, the sorrows of those will increase who run after other gods" (Ps. 16:2–4, author's paraphrase).

Without the Creator/creature distinction of biblical revelation, without a sense of the mystery and majesty of the person of God, there is no good thing but only an increase in sorrows: confusion, unholiness, impersonal emptiness, and final disintegration. The revelation of God, the transcendent triune Creator, stands at the heart of biblical faith, and thus at the heart of the gospel. It is at the beginning (Genesis) and at the end (Revelation) of biblical faith. Because biblical faith begins with the statement: "In the beginning God created the heavens and the earth" (Gen. 1:1), this is how ancient Israel worshiped throughout her history:

Come, let us bow down in worship,
let us kneel before the LORD our Maker. (Ps. 95:6)

This has not become old hat in the new covenant nor in its final expression, for the same worship of the beginning is to be found at the end. The twenty-four elders in heaven worship for all eternity, along with the church regnant, saying:

> You are worthy, our Lord and God, to receive glory and honor and power, for you created all things, and by your will they were created and have their being. (Rev. 4:11)

God the Creator has always been and will always be celebrated, because he is at the center of the gospel. The Creator is the Redeemer; the Maker is the Mender. Thus, the church militant now sings:

> *Praise God, from whom all blessings flow;*
> *Praise Him, all creatures here below;*
> *Praise Him above, ye heavenly host;*
> *Praise Father, Son, and Holy Ghost.*

We sing still, because the words of the prophet still are true and ever will be: "All men are like grass. . . . The grass withers and the flowers fall, but the word of our God stands forever" (Isa. 40:5–8).

3

One Savior

RICHARD D. PHILLIPS

For all have sinned and fall short of the glory of God, and are justified by his grace as a gift, through the redemption that is in Christ Jesus, whom God put forward as a propitiation by his blood, to be received by faith.

ROMANS 3:23-25

The previous chapter of this book documented the tectonic shift occurring on our religious landscape, threatening the biblical worldview on which Western civilization was built. One of the places where the moving fault lines are best felt is talk radio. My exposure to this occurred late one night when my computer software crashed. Driving to an all-night superstore in search of a fix, I tuned into "The Savage Nation"—Michael Savage's radio call-in show.

The topic that night was "spirituality," and though I listened only long enough to hear one conversation, it was certainly enlightening. The caller was a Buddhist. When Savage asked the man what he gained from his Buddhism, the man talked about helpful proverbial sayings—things like "don't let circumstances determine your attitude" and "it is better to be contented with what you have than to win great riches." This launched Savage on one of the diatribes that makes talk-radio what it is: "This proves that all religions are the same and we can take the best from each!"

It turns out that my computer had crashed while I was working on the material for this chapter on the exclusive claims of Jesus Christ as the one Savior. Via this radio show, I was providentially reminded of how passionately our relativistic world abhors the exclusive claims of Christ. "All the same!" insists the radio pundit. "Only Jesus!" the Christian replies. The doctrine of salvation by faith in Christ alone is not the only difference between Christianity and the spirituality of neopagan postmodernity. Nor is it the foundational difference, as Peter Jones instructed us in the previous chapter on the doctrine of God. But the Christian claim of "Christ alone!" is certainly where we come to the sharp edge of the blade in the contest between Christianity and the world.

What's the Problem?

In the movie *Grand Canyon* an affluent lawyer breaks out of a traffic jam and seeks an alternative route. The way he chooses becomes darker and more deserted, and just as he is reconsidering the wisdom of his action, his luxury car breaks down. Looking around, the lawyer finds himself in the kind of bad neighborhood he has only read about. Pulling out his cell phone, he calls a tow truck, but before it arrives five young thugs surround his car and threaten him with severe injuries. Just in time, the tow truck shows up. Its driver confidently walks up and starts hooking up to the car.

Naturally, the young hoodlums take offense at this: the man is interrupting a choice opportunity. So the truck driver pulls aside the leader of the gang and gives him a short education in ethics: "Man," he says, "the world ain't supposed to work like this. Maybe you don't know that, but this ain't the way it's supposed to be. I'm supposed to be able to do my job without askin' you if I can. And that dude is supposed to be able to wait with his car without you rippin' him off. Everything's supposed to be different than what it is here."[1]

---

[1] Cited from Cornelius Plantinga Jr., *Not the Way It's Supposed to Be: A Breviary of Sin* (Grand Rapids, MI: Eerdmans, 1995), 7.

This is something almost everyone is agreed about: that "everything's supposed to be different than what it is here." There is something wrong in the world. The question is, what is it? What is the problem facing mankind? This is important, because the nature of a problem always determines the nature of its solution. It is because of Christianity's and the Bible's answer to this question—why aren't things the way they're supposed to be?—that we proclaim Jesus Christ as the one and only Savior.

In the twentieth century, many people assumed that the main problem with people is *ignorance*. In underdeveloped nations, the people lacked the knowledge necessary to produce a modern economy, and even in America today we assign problems to ignorance. Why do people have hatred for others of a different race? Because they are unenlightened about racial equality; they have outdated ideas that need to be replaced. Why are young girls getting pregnant? Because they do not understand that there are ways of having sex without risking pregnancy. If ignorance is the problem, then the answer is *education*. At a more searching level, this is the approach of psychology: we don't understand what goes on in our minds, and by learning about these things we can better cope. Under this diagnosis of mankind's problem, we have dedicated enormous resources to education. But what is the result? Are things the way they are supposed to be? In fact, education has made things no better—and because of what we have taught people, education has in some respects made things quite worse.

Another approach of the past century was to identify the problem as poor environment. The cause of crime, we were told, is poverty. Many grow up in "dysfunctional" families and neighborhoods. The answer to this was *societal reengineering*. In the 1960s, the Lyndon B. Johnson administration launched *The Great Society*, the massive welfare institution with which most Americans today have grown up . But the result has been the breakdown of families and neighborhoods to a far greater degree than ever before. Moreover, even when we succeed in providing the environments we have wanted—for instance, in our brilliantly executed suburban paradises—things still are not the way they are supposed to be. The darkness and despair of our affluent, white, suburban youth belies the idea that the satiation of our lower needs will open the door for growth in the higher social and spiritual realms.

I happen to live in a suburban "paradise," where many people have enormous wealth and access to lifestyles of endless consumer delights. There, the problem many people identify is *mortality*. The baby boomers are now facing the uphill battle against age. Their beauty and vitality are fading away, so plastic surgery and weekly spa visits, expensive creams and new medical wonders are their hope for a fountain of youth.

In one way or another, all these are *modern* definitions of problems and solutions. They arise out of a worldview that sees man as good, powerful, and able so that we must simply progress forward. This explains the religious devotion of people to television shows like *Star Trek*, since they point to an age to come when mankind will have progressed to a higher plane. On the premise that mankind is basically good and able, modernity teaches that the problem is that we simply haven't had enough time yet. The solution to them all is *we're working on it*.

If this is true, it is an offense to state that Jesus Christ is the only Savior. Modernity demands that Jesus be reduced to only a teacher—one of many, however excellent he may be—and leaves no role for his work as Mediator between man and God. Since Christianity refuses to deny Christ as a mediatorial, atoning Savior, the world responds in anger. One typically modernist complaint put it this way: "Christianity is a contentious faith which requires an all-or-nothing commitment to Jesus as the one and only incarnation of the Son of God . . . [Christians are] uncompromising, ornery, militant, rigorous, imperious and invincibly

self-righteous."[2] Philip G. Ryken accurately names this a historically majority opinion among non-Christians: "For the past 2,000
years, Christianity's claims about the unique truth of Jesus Christ
have aroused no end of opposition from Jews, pagans, Muslims,
Communists, humanists, and atheists."[3]

We might think this situation is improved in light of the postmodern emphasis on "tolerance." It is true that *postmodernity*
introduces a new approach to defining mankind's basic problem,
largely in response to the obvious failure of the *modern* agendas.
Increasingly today, people lack confidence in the goodness and ability of man to work out his problems through reason and hard
work. Now, the problem is that man—specifically Western men
and women—are limited by their experience and outlook. In our
new global world, we need to profit from the wisdom of other cultures, especially from those pagan spiritualities found in the East.
What the East tells us is that we have erred through our commitment to *rationalism*. We must escape this through the solution of
mystic spirituality.

Paganism believes that all is one, without true hierarchy or
structure. The answer thus lies in the eradication of all distinctions
or the melding of opposites into new syntheses. Peter Jones tells us
that according to postmodern paganism, "we must rid the world
of distinctions and enter the mystical unity of all things." We must
stop distinguishing between the Creator and the creature, God and
man, animals and humans, right and wrong, life and death, heaven
and hell, the Bible and other sacred books, male and female, traditional families and alternative families, and children and parents,
to name just a few.[4] John Lennon summarized this in his anthem
for the postmodern, pagan world:

---

[2] Alan Watts, *Beyond Theology* (New York: World Publishing, 1967), *xii*.
[3] Philip Graham Ryken, *Is Jesus the Only Way?* (Wheaton, IL: Crossway, 1999), 11.
[4] Peter Jones, *Gospel Truth, Pagan Lies* (Escondido, CA: Main Entry Editions, 2004), 48–56.

Imagine there's no heaven
It's easy if you try
No hell below us
Above us only sky
Imagine all the people
Living life for today. . . .

You may say I'm a dreamer
But I'm not the only one
I hope someday you'll join us
And the world will live as one.[5]

If that is the dream, if what we need is to escape a falsely rational view of life and reality so as to achieve a subliminal, transcendent breakthrough, then the solution is to look within, turning from
the mind to the feelings, so as to achieve harmony and integration
with the oneness of all things. If this is true, then clearly it is a dangerous threat to suggest that one must turn in faith to the one Lord
and Savior revealed in the Bible in order to be saved. This becomes
the one rational vestige. In a society where this removal of distinctions and rejection of rational thought is increasingly embraced—
and so it is in our "tolerance"-obsessed culture—the idea that Christ
is the one and only Savior is an intolerable outrage and offense.

The Biblical Doctrine of Sin

I mentioned listening to the great theologian Michael Savage on the
radio. His caller was a Buddhist, who shared some Eastern proverbial wisdom. Predictably, Savage replied that this proves the unity
of all true religions. They all basically give the same message of getting in tune with your spirit and provide the same helpful wisdom
of the ages. But, he hastened to add, there was one false religion—
that which insists that faith in Jesus Christ is the only way to

---

[5] John Lennon, "Imagine," 1971.

heaven. Here is where the unity of all things stops, and here is where tolerance ends. The last time Savage had an evangelical Christian teaching the necessity of faith in Christ, he was proud to say, he intolerantly evicted the Christian from his studio. Listening to this, and marveling at the cultural education Savage was providing his nationwide audience, his Buddhist caller made the very point that was on my mind. As Savage was opining about the sameness of all religions, his caller interrupted, "Oh, there is one thing different about Buddhism. Buddhism does not believe in sin."

There it is! This shows us where the point of tension and offense really lies. What really separates Christianity from all other religions is not merely its doctrine of Christ, but its doctrine of sin. According to the Bible, the problem with this world—the reason things aren't the way they're supposed to be—is sin, that is, the transgression of God's law and the power of evil that thus takes residence in our hearts.

This is Paul's point in Romans 3:23. Why is Jesus the one and only Savior? Paul says, "For all have sinned and fall short of the glory of God." It is the nature of the problem that specifies the nature of the solution, and the offense of Christianity is its insistence that sin, biblically defined, is the true problem of mankind. Unless we accept sin as our problem, says Cornelius Plantinga, "the idea that the human race needs a Savior sounds quaint."[6] Indeed, it increasingly sounds outrageous and offensive.

In his valuable book on sin, *Not the Way It's Supposed to Be*, Plantinga explains why sin is the true reason things are not as they are supposed to be. The first reason is that "sin distorts our character, a central feature of our very humanity. Sin corrupts powerful human capacities—thought, emotion, speech, and act—so that they become centers of attack on others or of defection or neglect."[7]

[6] Plantinga, *xiii*.
[7] Ibid., 2.

This is the very point made by Paul in Romans. When he says, "All have sinned," he includes the idea that we are corrupted by sin. "None is righteous, no, not one; no one understands; no one seeks for God. . . . No one does good, not even one" (Rom. 3:10–12). The problem is within our nature, Paul says, and then is manifested in our thoughts, desires, and actions. We are not the people we were meant to be; we have gone wrong; a corruption has entered humanity at the very level of our nature. Martyn Lloyd-Jones writes:

> We think, because we dress differently and have cars and aeroplanes and bombs, that we are essentially different from everybody who has ever lived before. But we are not! We are exactly what men and women have always been. We are still sinners, we are still failures. However great our learning may be, we are governed by lusts and prejudices and ideas and passions. We remain the same.[8]

Already, we can see that if this is true, if sin is the problem which corrupts our very nature, then no change in environment is going to solve our predicament. This is why education, while laudible in itself, does not work; being corrupt we teach corrupt things. The same goes for societal engineering. If we are the problem, then the solution cannot be "we are working on it." We need someone else to work on our problem—someone not corrupted by sin— which is the very good news that Christianity proclaims. When Christians say that Jesus Christ is the one and only Savior, we mean that Jesus is the sinless Savior who is uniquely able to solve the problems that our efforts can only make worse.

But there is another way in which sin is the problem that demands only Christ as its solution. Sin not only corrupts us, but it also causes the anger of God toward us. Here is something that

---

[8] D. Martyn Lloyd-Jones, *Love So Amazing: Expositions of Colossians 1* (Grand Rapids, MI: Baker, 1995), 65.

the postmodern pagan cannot abide. It is merely assumed that God is at our service. God is for us unless we are some obviously hell-deserving person like Osama bin Laden or the presidential candidate of the opposing political party. But the Bible teaches otherwise. Paul's long presentation of the gospel in Romans begins with this statement of the problem: "For the wrath of God is revealed from heaven against all ungodliness and unrighteousness of men" (Rom. 1:18). Sin is the problem because it alienates us from the Almighty: it changes our relationship with God so that instead of the benevolent favor that postmoderns assume, we receive the wrathful hostility of an offended holy deity.

If there is one shift that has taken place in evangelical teaching and preaching, it involves the downplaying of God's wrath as the result of our sin and, reciprocally, the downplaying of the value of the shed blood of Jesus Christ. David Wells points out that surveys indicate only 17 percent of evangelicals think of sin as an offense to God or as a cause of guilt before the divine seat of judgment. Sin is about ways we do harm to one another; it is not something that actually causes God to be hostile towards us. We talk of sin only on the horizontal axis: sin is "human relational adjustment dynamics."[9] Lately, things are getting even worse. James Davison Hunter points out that today "the word *sin* . . . now finds its home mostly on dessert menus. 'Peanut Butter Binge' and 'Chocolate Challenge' are sinful; lying is not."[10]

I have been approvingly citing Cornelius Plantinga's book on sin. But I could not help noticing that even this book-length discussion of sin downplays the reality of God's wrath. The index reveals no headings for the words guilt, wrath, judgment, or hell, and this is an evangelical, Reformed book wholly devoted to the doctrine of sin.

---

[9] Plantinga, x.
[10] Ibid.

It is far worse in the mainstream press. Rabbi Harold Kushner recently published a book titled *How Good Do We Have to Be?* Its premise is that God accepts us just as we are, and that we need to get beyond out-dated ideas of guilt. The first chapter is titled "God Loves You Anyway." It opens with Kushner's reflection on the Yom Kippur crowds at his synagogue, most of whom come seeking forgiveness for sins. But Kushner explains why this is wrong: "It is the notion that we were supposed to be perfect . . . that leaves us constantly feeling guilty." So he corrects this error: "The fundamental message of religion is not that we are sinners because we are not perfect, but that the challenge of being human is so complex that God knows better than to expect perfection from us."[11] To argue this, Kushner presents a creative interpretation of Genesis 3 that says God put the tree of the knowledge of good and evil in the garden because he wanted us to break his command, since only in autonomous freedom can humans ever mature beyond notions of guilt and sin.

I find this basic attitude played out in the piety of many Christians. It wasn't that long ago when a Christian who sinfully neglected his marriage, to the point where his spouse separates or sues for divorce, would cringe before the idea of God's displeasure. He would ask, how can God accept me back into his presence? But that is not the response I hear today. Now, evangelicals agree with Rabbi Kushner: "God loves me anyway." What I hear now is, how can God let me down like this? Gone is David's plea to God: "Against you, you only, have I sinned" (Ps. 51:4). God is not there to judge me but only to help me, and why isn't he doing a better job?

But Paul is emphatic: God's wrath is revealed against human unrighteousness. "The wages of sin is death" (Rom. 6:23). He tells

---

[11] Harold Kushner, *How Good Do We Have to Be? A New Understanding of Guilt and Forgiveness* (New York: Little Brown, 1996), 8, 10.

us we have sinned precisely in that we are not perfect as God designed and demands: "All have sinned and fall short of the glory of God" (Rom. 3:23). This is the ultimate reason why sin is our true problem. Yes, sin corrupts our nature, and sin makes our lives miserable. But more important than these, the guilt of sin incurs God's righteous, holy wrath. "It is a fearful thing to fall into the hands of the living God" (Heb. 10:31). "Do not fear those who kill the body but cannot kill the soul," Jesus said. "Rather fear him who can destroy both soul and body in hell" (Matt. 10:28).

Donald Grey Barnhouse demonstrated God's wrath in a sermon titled *Men Whom God Struck Dead*. He reminded us of Nadab and Abihu, the sons of the first high priest, Aaron. They were well-spoken of in Scripture until they entered the tabernacle and offered "unauthorized fire" before the Lord. We are not told exactly what this was, except that it was different from what God had commanded (Lev. 10:1). There is every indication that they were well-meaning, if inattentive. Leviticus 10:2 tells us what happened: "Fire came out from before the LORD and consumed them, and they died before the LORD." God explained: "Among those who are near me I will be sanctified" (10:3).

Barnhouse moves on to Uzzah, a man who was struck dead by God when David was trying to bring the ark of the covenant up to Jerusalem. David had put the ark on an ox cart, contrary to God's clear instructions. At one point the oxen stumbled and the ark threatened to topple off the cart. Uzzah "put out his hand to the ark of God and took hold of it" to keep it from falling into the dirt. "And the anger of the Lord was kindled against Uzzah, and God struck him down there because of his error, and he died there beside the ark of God" (2 Sam. 6:6–7).

Lastly, Barnhouse remembers the fate of Ananias and Sapphira, who lied to the apostle Peter about the amount of money they had given to the church. God struck them both dead on the spot. Peter explained, "You have . . . lied to God" (Acts 5:4).

Barnhouse points out that these were believers! Yet God struck them dead for offending his holiness: two for inaccurate worship in the tabernacle, one for touching the holy ark with his unholy hand, and two for lying to God before the church. The situation is certainly no better for unbelievers who offend God. Achan broke God's command by keeping silver, a cloak, and a bar of gold from the destroyed city of Jericho. God, in his "burning anger," had Achan, along with his sons and daughters and his oxen and donkeys and sheep and his tent, taken into the Valley of Achor. There, they were all burned with fire, stoned to death, and buried under a great heap of rocks (Josh. 7:24–25).

This picture of a savagely just God, of a holy, demanding deity who keeps precise records and judges accordingly, does not play very well on talk radio. But he is the God of the Bible. The point truly is not that something is wrong with this picture of God, but that something truly is wrong with sin. Sin is our great problem, and therefore the solution must take away our sin and turn aside God's wrath. Lloyd-Jones explains, "The great obstacle . . . is the obstacle of sin; sin in general and sins in particular. It is our sins that have come between us and God . . . So . . . something has to be done about this problem of our sin and our sins. It was to perform this special and particular work that the Son of God came into this world."[12]

Paul says in Romans 3:24 that our redemption is "in Christ Jesus," that is, through faith in his saving work. Jesus' shed blood is the "propitiation" for God's wrath against our sin; by dying on our behalf, Jesus satisfies God's just anger so that it is turned away from us. Only he, the divine Son of God, can do this, so he is the one Savior who can save us from the problem of our sins. "Behold, the lamb of God, who takes away the sin of the world" (John 1:29),

---

[12] D. Martyn Lloyd-Jones, *God's Ultimate Purpose* (Grand Rapids, MI: Baker, 1978), 148.

said John the Baptist, and the Christian gospel is steadfast in continuing to point to him alone for salvation from sin.

One Savior: The Glorious Work of Jesus Christ

This leads us to a second and more positive reason why Jesus is the one and only Savior: because of the singularly glorious and wonderful character of his saving work for us. When secularists complain about Christian exclusivity—that Christians teach that you must believe what we believe or suffer forever in hell—we should object to this as a grotesque perversion of the most glorious and wonderful good news ever heard on this earth. That the glorious gospel of God's only Son should be maligned so perversely is itself an exposé of the evil of sin.

Think of what the angels said when Jesus was born: "Glory to God in the highest, and on earth peace among those with whom he is pleased!" (Luke 2:14). The incarnation of Christ is itself stupendously good news. The Son of God was born into this world so that he can show us how to live. He was born with human emotions and will so that he can sympathize with our feelings. But, most important, God the Son was born in a human frame so that he could die. So when people complain against any special claims regarding Jesus Christ, they object to the most stupendous and glorious thing God has ever done: he sent his Son into this world to teach us heavenly truth, to sympathize with us as God in the flesh, but especially to die in our place on the cross.

It is the last of these that Paul emphasizes. He says that Jesus redeemed us from sin at the cost of his blood. There is a story in the Old Testament that explains what this is about. God used the prophet Hosea to provide an example of his redeeming grace through Jesus Christ. He told Hosea to marry a certain woman, Gomer, who proved to be unfaithful. She pursued her lovers and descended further into sin, but Hosea remained steadfast in his love for her. But just as it does for us, sin made Gomer a slave; literally,

she ended upon on the auction block to be sold, probably because
of debts. God told Hosea, her husband, to buy her back to demonstrate his own faithful love for us. Slaves were typically sold in the
town square, stripped naked for all to inspect. This is the same
degradation into which sin seeks to drag us all.

The men gathered to place bids on the body of this female slave.
"Twelve pieces of silver," bid one. "Thirteen," called a voice from
the back she may no longer have remembered. "Fourteen," came the
reply. "Fifteen," said Hosea. "Fifteen silver pieces and a bushel of
barley." Stepping forward and reaching out to his wife, Hosea
spoke, "Fifteen pieces of silver and a bushel and a half of barley."
Everyone realized he could not be outbid and so the other men
began to walk away. She was rightly his already, but sin had torn
her away. Now he had bought her back with everything he had and
then he draped her with his love: "So I bought her for fifteen shekels
of silver and a homer and a lethek of barley. Then I told her, 'You
are to live with me many days; you must not be a prostitute or be
intimate with any man, and I will live with you'" (Hos. 3:2–3).

This is what Jesus came into this world to do for us. James
Boice comments, "We were created for intimate fellowship with
God and for freedom, but we have disgraced ourselves by unfaith-
fulness. First we have flirted with and then committed adultery with
this sinful world and its values. The world even bid for our soul,
offering sex, money, fame, power and all the other items in which
it traffics. But Jesus, our faithful bridegroom and lover, entered the
marketplace to buy us back. He bid his own blood. There is no
higher bid than that. And we became his. He reclothed us, not in
the wretched rags of our old unrighteousness, but in his new robes
of righteousness. He has said to us, 'You must dwell as mine . . .
you shall not belong to another . . . so will I also be to you.'"[13]

---

[13] James M. Boice, *Foundations of the Christian Faith* (Downers Grove, IL: InterVarsity,
1986), 329–30.

Only Jesus can redeem us from sin, and he purchases us for his love at the cost of his own infinite blood. Far from repudiating the singular glory of this redemption, which none other would or could provide since Jesus alone is untouched by the stain and corruption of sin, we should embrace it with the highest joy. We should sing, "Love so amazing, so divine / demands my life, my soul, my all." But if we reject this sole Redeemer, we can only remain in the bondage of our sin, ultimately to reap the wages of sin that is death. The writer of Hebrews rightly answers the denial that Jesus is the one Savior by asking, "How shall we escape if we neglect such a great salvation?" (Heb. 2:3).

One Savior: The Sole Provision of a Gracious God

Finally, Christians insist that Jesus Christ is the one and only Savior, apart from whom we must perish, because he is the sole provision of a gracious God for our reconciliation with him.

We are the ones who have sinned against God. That was true in the Garden and it is true today. God has not sinned against us. Therefore it is God who will dictate the terms of reconciliation with him. That there are any terms at all, that there is any way for sinners to come to God, is an instance of amazing grace. But how impertinent it is of us, since we are the guilty offenders, to insist that we have the right to determine the way we will come to God. Yet this is precisely the position of those who deny Jesus as the one Savior.

Is Jesus the one way God has established? Everywhere today we hear, "There are many ways to God." Let us observe, at least, that Jesus taught the exact opposite. There are many ways to hell, he said, but only one way to God: "The gate is wide and the way is easy that leads to destruction, and those who enter by it are many. For the gate is narrow and the way is hard that leads to life, and those who find it are few" (Matt. 7:13–14). What, then, is that singular way that leads to life? Jesus said, "I am the way, and the truth, and the life. No one comes to the Father except through me" (John 14:6). Perhaps that is just a son's boasting. But John 3:16–18 confirms it from God's own appointment: "For God so loved the world, that he gave his only Son, that whoever believes in him should not perish but have eternal life. . . . Whoever believes in him is not condemned, but whoever does not believe is condemned already." The right response to this is not to repudiate it, not to insist on finding your own way to God, but to look to Jesus Christ in faith so as to be forgiven of your sins and to enter into eternal life with God.

This very point was dramatized in the fourth chapter of the Bible. Adam and Eve's sons, Cain and Abel, both sought to come to God:

> Now Abel was a keeper of sheep, and Cain a worker of the ground. In the course of time Cain brought to the LORD an offering of the fruit of the ground, and Abel also brought of the firstborn of his flock and of their fat portions. And the LORD had regard for Abel and his offering, but for Cain and his offering he had no regard. (Gen. 4:2–5)

This is enormously instructive, because here we have two brothers with eminent lineage, who both sincerely sought to come to God for the purpose of worship. But they came in two different ways: one by the fruit of his labors, that is by human works, and the other by the sacrifice of an innocent animal. Each might have thought along the way: I am coming to God by the way that seems right to me, so he is sure to receive and bless me. But that is not what happened. God only accepted ("had regard for") one of the brothers' offerings.

It turns out that Abel's offering matched the way that God had taught his parents to come to him—through the blood of a sacrificial offering, which pointed forward to Jesus Christ in his saving death on the cross (see Gen. 3:21). Even then, Jesus was the only way sinners could come to God; all others were rejected and refused. This is what Paul taught in Romans 3:23–25: "All have sinned and fall short of the glory of God, and are justified by his grace as a gift, through the redemption that is in Christ Jesus, whom God put forward as a propitiation by his blood, to be received by faith." This is the way that God has so graciously provided, at such great cost to himself and to his only Son, and it is the only way by which we may be received into his favor for blessing.

No Other Name

In his sermon "Men Whom God Struck Dead," Donald Grey Barnhouse vividly recalls biblical proofs of God's swift wrath against sin. But he points out as well that the same God, when his wrath has been dealt with by the one Savior whom he has provided—even his own Son who came to bear our sins upon the cross—receives even the worst sinners into his loving affection. Barnhouse writes:

> If we look through the Bible, we find that many of the men who were guilty of some of the worst offences not only were not struck dead by God but, apparently, were readily forgiven and raised to places of highest usefulness afterwards. [Examples of this include Abraham, who cravenly lied and sacrificed the honor of his wife to protect his life.] Yet later he was greatly used by God and was called "the friend of God." Moses was a murderer and a fugitive. Then God dealt with him, bringing him back, and empowering him to lead his people from bondage to freedom. . . . David compounded murder to protect his adultery. Then God called him a man after his own heart, singing the most beautiful hymns of history through his lips. Peter denied the Lord Jesus Christ, not for money, as Judas did, but for fear of the words of a servant girl. Yet the risen Lord commissioned him to use the keys to open the Kingdom—first, at Pentecost, to the Jews and then, in the house of Cornelius, to the Gentiles.[14]

---

[14] Donald Grey Barnhouse, *Men Whom God Struck Dead* (Philadelphia: Alliance of Confessing Evangelicals, 2004), 1–2.

This tells us two essential things. First, those who recognize and confess their sin, having realized their desperate predicament before God, have no complaint that he has provided only one Savior. A man dying of thirst in the desert does not complain to stumble upon only one spring of life-giving water. A man dying of cancer does not object that there is only one person who donates the blood marrow that matches his own and saves his life. And a sinner, gazing upon the otherwise unavoidable prospect of unremitting corruption in this life and just, eternal condemnation in the life to come, does not object to the Lord Jesus Christ—the Son of God who lovingly bore for us the hell our sin deserves—and say, "Why must my soul be saved in only this way?" This makes the point that the unbelieving world's true objection to Jesus Christ as the one Savior is really an objection to God's verdict of sin. What they object to doing is confess their sin. What they demand is another way—any other way—that grants a salvation that is to their own glory instead of to God's.

It may be true that all the world's various, self-appointed roads equally lead to God. But the horror that they will discover, if God's Word is true, is that the God to whom they arrive by those ways is an angry, offended, and awesomely holy God. And they will call out to the mountains and rocks, "Fall on us and hide us from the face of him who is seated on the throne, and from the wrath of the Lamb, for the great day of their wrath has come, and who can stand?" (Rev. 6:16–17). I pray that you will not be among that number, that you will now accept God's verdict upon you—that you have sinned and fall short of the glory of God and justly deserve his condemnation. I pray that you will turn to the one solution for this greatest of problems, rejoice at the singularly wonderful work of the Lord Jesus Christ for you, and come to God by the one way his grace has provided, and through the one Savior, Jesus Christ, you will be saved.

Lastly, this tells us that when we do come to Jesus Christ in faith,

God's grace has wonderful gifts for us. We are justified by his grace as a gift. We are redeemed by the purchase of Christ's blood. God's wrath is turned away by that same blood. What, then, for those who submit to God's one Savior? Jesus said, "If the Son sets you free, you will be free indeed" (John 8:36). We are then free to live apart from sin by the power of the Spirit Jesus sends. We are free to serve him, each according to our calling but all of us through our witness to the gospel. And when our earthly pilgrimage leads through this life into the next, we are free to enter the city of God for an eternity of glory. "Blessed are those who wash their robes," Jesus said, "so that they"—and they alone—"have the right to the tree of life and that they may enter the city by the gates" (Rev. 22:14).

There is only one way into that city, and only one way to be free from the condemnation of sin that is the bane of our human condition. But that one way—that one Savior Jesus Christ—is enough; indeed, he brings an infinity of God's grace for an eternity of joy and peace and love. So we, the Christian church, following the apostolic witness, as taught by the Lord Jesus Christ, boldly and joyfully affirm, "There is salvation in no one else, for there is no other name under heaven given among men by which we must be saved" (Acts 4:12).

4

One Truth

PHILIP G. RYKEN

Jesus answered, "You say that I am a king. For this purpose I was born and for this purpose I have come into the world—to bear witness to the truth. Everyone who is of the truth listens to my voice." Pilate said to him, "What is truth?"

JOHN 18:37–38

At a time of deep discouragement and desperate danger, when there were enemies on every side and God was the only hope he had left, the psalmist gave this plaintive cry: "If the foundations are destroyed, what can the righteous do?" (Ps. 11:3). In posing this question, he assumed that when a foundation is destroyed, everything else will come tumbling down with it.

Today the foundations are under attack. It would be hard to think of even a single major doctrine of the Christian faith that is not under attack in these postmodern times. The doctrine of God (which is attacked by open theism), the doctrine of Scripture (which is undermined by doubts about inerrancy), the doctrine of the atonement (which is destroyed by the denial of our need for a blood substitute), the doctrine of justification (which is redefined and thus disabled by new perspectives on Paul and the law)—everything seems to be under attack. But no attack is more fundamental than the attack on truth itself, the assault on the very claim that some things are true and others are false.

Consider a telling statistic. More than a decade ago, George Barna showed that scarcely 50 percent of those who identify themselves as evangelical Christians believe that there are moral or intellectual absolutes.[1] That was alarming enough, but more recent data is even scarier: only 9 percent of evangelical students now believe in anything called "absolute truth."[2] The rest are students who say they believe in the Bible as the Word of God, and profess to have saving faith in Jesus Christ, but do not believe in the truth of truth.

This fundamental weakness in the contemporary church is part of wider cultural trends. As Os Guinness has observed, "A solid sense of truth is foundering in America at large. Vaporized by critical theories, obscured by clouds of euphemism and jargon, outpaced by humor and hype, overlooked for style and image, and eroded by advertising, truth in America is anything but marching on." And then Guinness makes this telling indictment: "With magnificent exceptions, evangelicals reflect this truth-decay and reinforce it. . . . Contemporary evangelicals are no longer people of truth."[3] If the foundations are thus destroyed, what then can the righteous do?

What Pilate Asked

The attack on truth is hardly a new phenomenon. It is nearly as old as the world itself, going all the way back to the garden, when Satan introduced the first doubt: "Did God *actually* say, 'You shall not eat of any tree in the garden'?" (Gen. 3:1; emphasis added). But perhaps the best Bible passage to help explain the current situation

---

[1] George Barna, *The Barna Report: What Americans Believe* (Ventura, CA: Regal, 1991), 292–94.
[2] Quoted in Charles Colson, "Worldview Boot Camp," *Christianity Today* (December 2004), 80.
[3] Os Guinness and John Seel, eds., *No God but God* (Chicago: Moody, 1992), 18.

comes from the Gospel of John, chapter 18, and the night when Jesus was betrayed.

Jesus went through more than one trial that night, first appearing before the Jewish Sanhedrin before being led to the palace of Pontius Pilate, the Roman governor. Pilate was no friend of the Jews (particularly at that hour of the morning!). So when he saw their prisoner, he asked them to state their business: "What accusation do you bring against this man?" (John 18:29). Actually, the Jewish leaders had the same question themselves. They had been up all night trying to figure out exactly what crime Jesus had committed. All they knew was that they wanted to get rid of him, but since they weren't quite sure what Pilate would consider legitimate grounds for a conviction, they gave a sly answer: "If this man were not doing evil, we would not have delivered him over to you" (John 18:30).

This was a way of alleging that Jesus was a criminal without actually stating what his crime was. Already we are beginning to see how slippery the truth can be in the hands of sneaky sinners. But Pilate was not deceived. Matthew says "he knew it was out of envy that they had delivered him up" (Matt. 27:18). So the governor told the priests to judge Jesus according to their own laws. However, this suggestion did not satisfy the priests because it did not achieve their real objective, which was to execute the death penalty. Even if they judged Jesus according to their own laws, as Pilate suggested, they didn't have the authority to carry out capital punishment. "It is not lawful for us to put anyone to death," they complained (John 18:31).

By this point Pilate realized that it was not going to be as easy as he had hoped to get rid of the mob outside his palace and go back to bed. He was going to have to figure out what the truth was. So to get to the bottom of it, he summoned Jesus inside and started to conduct his own investigation. "Are you the King of the Jews?" he asked (John 18:33). "What have you done?" (John 18:35). Pilate wanted to know the truth.

Jesus gave the governor some honest answers. He *was* a king,
but not the kind that Pilate was used to. "My kingdom," he said,
"is not of this world" (John 18:36). For a moment it seemed like
Pilate had the answer he was looking for: "So you are a king." And
of course it was true, so Jesus said, "You say that I am a king. For
this purpose I was born and for this purpose I have come into the
world—to bear witness to the truth. Everyone who is of the truth
listens to my voice" (John 18:37).

These were staggering claims. Jesus was claiming the rights of
kingship. He was saying that he had come from somewhere outside the world for a special divine purpose. He was claiming to
speak the truth *and* he was claiming that anyone who wanted to
know the truth should listen to him. Jesus was doing more than
standing up for the truth; he was claiming to be its personal agent.
Furthermore, he was claiming to be the supreme arbiter of truth in
the world. Knowing the difference between what is true and what
is false, therefore, depends on listening to what Jesus says.

All of this was more than Pilate was ready or willing to accept.
So he raised his famous question: "What is truth?" (John 18:38).
Maybe he said this in frustration, the way that people do during a
trial when they despair of ever finding out what really happened.
Maybe he said it with an air of breezy dismissal. Maybe he snorted
with indignation at the very idea that anyone would claim to know
the absolute truth. But however he said it, Pilate refused to wait
around for the answer. Sir Francis Bacon captured the scene perfectly in the opening words of his famous essay on the subject of
truth: "*What is truth?* said jesting Pilate, and would not stay for an
answer."[4] Bacon had read his Gospels, because after the governor
asked his famous question Pilate did not stay, but "went back outside to the Jews" (John 18:38). To know what the truth is, sometimes a person has to wait around for the answer, but Pilate didn't

---

[4] Francis Bacon, "Of Truth," *Essays or Counsels—Civil and Moral*, Harvard Classics, 3 (New York: Collier, 1909), 7.

do that. Although he asked the question, he didn't really expect an answer. His question was only rhetorical—his way of putting off making a commitment.

Pontius Pilate would have felt right at home in these postmodern times. Here was a man who at some level wanted to know the truth. He was even conducting an investigation into the truth. But when he was confronted with Jesus Christ and the claims of absolute truth, he began to question whether it was really possible to know the truth after all. In the end, rather than seeing the argument through to a place of resolution, he gave up on the quest for truth altogether.

People do the same thing today. They are curious enough to investigate religion, and at some point they will probably come into contact with Jesus Christ, as Pilate did. But when they start hearing the claims of Christianity, they are quick to raise objections about the possibility that anyone can really know the truth. This is a response that strikes at the very foundations. And it is a response that is being made with renewed force in our day, when there is radical skepticism about the knowledge of absolute truth.

No Place for Truth

Today we are witnessing a world-changing shift in epistemology from the modern to the postmodern.[5] The modern worldview was confident "that human beings, beginning with themselves and their own methods of knowing, could gain an understanding of the world."[6] The modernist takes a single, unified view of the world and tries to bring order and understanding to human experience. When we think of modernism, we need to think of totalizing systems that organize knowable reality according to basic principles— systems like Marxism or Darwinism. Pose Pilate's question ("What

---

[5] Simply put, epistemology is the study of how we know things.

[6] David K. Naugle, *Worldview: The History of a Concept* (Grand Rapids, MI: Eerdmans, 2002), 173–74.

is truth?") and a modernist will tell you that we are perpetrators or victims of economic exploitation (Marxism), or that we are the product of a random evolutionary process that did not have us in mind (Darwinism). That is the truth.

The proponents of these modern systems believed that prosperity, peace, and justice were within the grasp of human reason, through science. Rational planning, applied technology, and social manipulation would solve our social problems.[7] One man who witnessed this attempt firsthand was Vaclav Havel, the former president of the Czech Republic. Writing in the *New York Times* not long after the fall of communism in Eastern Europe, Havel described modernism as "the proud belief that man, as the pinnacle of everything that exists, was capable of objectively describing, explaining and controlling everything that exists, and of possessing the one and only truth about the world."[8]

Make no mistake: this modern worldview is still with us. Nevertheless, and at the same time, we are witnessing the rise of a new way of looking at the world that is generally identified as postmodernism, which may simply be described as intellectual relativism. With the rise of postmodernism, "confidence in humanity as an objective, omnicompetent knower has been smashed, destroying any hopes of ascertaining the truth about the universe."[9] There is no one right way of looking at the world; your worldview is just your opinion.

The confrontation between the modern and the postmodern worldview is aptly depicted in two men who meet face-to-face on a street corner in one of Wiley Miller's *Non Sequitur* comics. One of the men is wearing a placard that says, "THE FACTS AS THEY ARE," while the other has a sign that reads, "THE

---

[7] Gene E. Veith, "Postmodern Times," *Modern Reformation* (September–October 1995), 16–19.
[8] Vaclav Havel, "The End of the Modern Era," *New York Times* (March 1, 1992), §4, 15.
[9] Naugle, 172.

TRUTH AS I SEE IT." [10] The man holding to the facts as they are is a modernist. He has an objective view of the world that is based, he thinks, on the way things actually are. The man defending the truth as he sees it is a man for postmodern times. His truth depends on his perspective.

These two worldviews represent ideas that have been building for centuries, and have now become part of daily life. Today we are likely to meet both of them on the same street corner. In fact, sometimes we meet them both in the same person. *Both* views pose a challenge to the Christian faith—one by giving an alternate truth, the other by saying there is no truth at all. But postmodernism lodges its attack at the very foundations. Modernism objected to Christianity on the grounds that it wasn't true, so at least people could still argue about what the truth was. But postmodernism says that different things can be true for different people. So people can accept that Christianity is true for someone else, in some sense, without accepting that it's true for them as well.

What else does postmodernism say about the truth? Postmodernism says that there is no truth, with a capital *T*. It is not merely skeptical about knowing the truth, but denies that there *is* any one absolute and universal truth to be known at all. After centuries of struggling to determine what we know and how we know it, many people are giving up on the very idea of objective truth altogether. Truth is subjective; what is most real and most true is my own experience. In America this kind of intellectual relativism has now been legally enshrined in the 1992 Supreme Court decision *Planned Parenthood v. Casey*, which stated that each person possesses "the right to define one's own concept of existence, of meaning, of the universe, and of the mystery of human life." [11] There is therefore "nothing deep down inside us except what we

---

[10] Wiley Miller, *Non Sequitur* (May 16, 1997).
[11] *Planned Parenthood v. Casey*, 505 U.S. 833 (1992).

have put there ourselves . . . no standard of rationality that is not obedient to our own conventions."[12] Truth, like beauty, is in the eye of the beholder.

Postmodernism holds that there is no single, objective, overarching perspective that gives us a true and comprehensive explanation of the world. There is no all-encompassing worldview. There are no facts, only interpretations. There is no ultimate reality, only different perspectives that make up different realities. There is no knowable correspondence between what we think and what is really there. Therefore, truth is not something we uncover, but only something we construct. This is even the case with a field like history, which a consistent postmodernist views as another form of fiction. There are no facts, only interpretations, each of which is equally valid. We are thus witnessing what Gertrude Himmelfarb has described as the "denial of the fixity of the past, of the reality of the past apart from what the historian chooses to make of it."[13]

Furthermore, postmodernism holds that what we believe to be true is determined by our cultural location. We only believe what we believe because of our gender, our ethnicity, or our social context. In another *Non Sequitur* comic strip, a child at a chalkboard has posted an unconventional answer to a basic problem of arithmetic: "2 + 2 = 17." The teacher glares disapprovingly, but the child has one last desperate line of defense: "Perhaps," he says, "the discrepancy between the answer I gave and the answer you want is due to our cultural or socio-economic differences . . ."[14] Most people still recognize that the truths of mathematics are not culturally determined. However, many people now believe that many other areas of truth *are* culture specific. If someone advocates a particu-

---

[12] Richard Rorty, quoted in James Sire, *The Universe Next Door: A Basic Worldview Catalog*, 4th ed. (Downers Grove, IL: InterVarsity, 2004), 227.
[13] Gertrude Himmelfarb, "Tradition and Creativity in the Writing of History," *First Things* (November 1992), 28.
[14] Wiley Miller, *Non Sequitur* (September 23, 1997).

lar approach to global politics, they say, for example, "You only think that way because you're an American." Or a particular stand on sexual ethics is dismissed because the person who holds it is a male, for example, or a heterosexual.

Postmodernism also says that people who claim to know the truth are only using it to advance their own personal or political agenda. It's all a power play. The reason people claim to know the truth is so that they can impose their views on others. It is the belief in absolute truth, they say, that leads to tyranny and oppression, whether religious or political. The only worldviews that are wrong are the ones that claim to know the truth. But they are not merely wrong; they are also dangerous, hence all the comparisons the media makes between evangelical Christianity and Islamic fundamentalism.

Not surprisingly, since postmodernism rejects the absolute truth, it is also anti-authoritarian. Whereas modernism tried to impose its authority (think of Darwinism's tyranny over public education in America), postmodernism tries to resist authority in all its forms. The slogan from the television program *X-Files* is characteristically postmodern: "Trust no one." This is one of the things that attracts people to postmodernism: it allows them to live in their own reality, with their own set of rules. It is the perfect worldview for the radical individualism of our culture.

Another characteristic of postmodernism is often described as "the revolt against the metanarrative." A narrative is simply a story, and a metanarrative is a grand story that ties everything together. Modernism is full of metanarratives. Marxism tells the story of class struggle; Darwinism tells the story of evolution; and so forth. Christianity has an alternative metanarrative, as we will see momentarily. But postmodernism is hostile to any narrative that tries to explain everything, Christianity included. Postmodernism tries to deconstruct any meaningful account of the universe. It says "there is no timeless certainty about knowledge of anything; there are no foundational truths that are universally true for any rational person."[15] As David Wells has said in his shattering critique of the contemporary church, there is no place for truth.[16]

Problems with Postmodernism

There is some truth to the postmodern critique of modern thought. As Christians we can agree with postmodernism that our perspective has an influence on what we believe, that our place in the world has an effect on what we know. We can also agree that sometimes we believe what we want to believe, and that, for reasons of our own purpose, we try to get other people to believe what we want them to believe, too. Our knowledge of the truth is not pristine, but like everything else in the world, it is corrupted by sin. As Christians, we know the limits of the fallen mind. We cannot know as perfectly or as completely as God knows. But that is not to say that we cannot know the truth at all. However incomplete and imperfect our knowledge is, it nevertheless corresponds to reality. We can know some things, to some extent, as they truly are.

Yet for all its insights, postmodernism must be recognized as an attack on the very foundations of truth, and we must join the battle at the very place where truth is under attack. There are serious problems with radical intellectual relativism. First, there is a logical problem: the claim that there are no absolutes is self-refuting. In other words, it contradicts itself. When people deny that there is any such thing as absolute truth, what they are really doing is introducing another absolute truth, namely, the absolute truth that there is no absolute truth! The position is self-refuting.

Once again, this point can be illustrated from *Non Sequitur*. A man walks down the street holding a sign that reads "There are no absolutes in life." It is a sign for these postmodern times, when

---

[15] Rodney Clapp, *Families at the Crossroads* (Downers Grove, IL: InterVarsity, 1993), 177.
[16] See David F. Wells, *No Place for Truth, or, Whatever Happened to Evangelical Theology?* (Grand Rapids, MI: Eerdmans, 1993).

truth is considered to be relative. But there is at least one onlooker who refuses to let the sign go unchallenged. A mild-mannered businessman peers around the corner of a building and says, "Uh-oh . . . looks like a job for . . . OBVIOUSMAN." He rips off his coat and tie to reveal his superhero costume: a purple leotard with the word "DUH" written across the chest and then crossed out. OBVIOUSMAN leaps in front of the sign-carrying postmodernist and says, "Hold it right there, you semantic ne'er-do-well. . . . Your sign makes an *absolute* statement, thus contradicting your so-called beliefs!" Then as he soars into the sky, a group of grateful bystanders say, "Thank you, OBVIOUSMAN!!"[17]

Well, we ought to be grateful whenever somebody points out an intellectual inconsistency, and when it comes to postmodernism, there is plenty of work for "OBVIOUSMAN" to do. Consider another example. The virtue postmodernism prizes the most is tolerance: everyone ought to accept everyone else's worldview as being true for them. But on what basis can the relativist say that anyone *ought* to do anything? If there are no absolutes, then not even tolerance can be defended as an absolute. As soon as we start using the language of moral obligation, we are claiming that there is an objective moral truth that is binding for everyone. But this is precisely what postmodernism denies. So who is the relativist to demand that anyone ought to do anything, including being tolerant of other worldviews?

Steven Turner shows the irony of all this in "Creed," his tongue-in-cheek confession of the postmodern faith:

> *We believe that all religions are basically the same*
> *At least the one that we read was.*
> *They all believe in love and goodness.*
> *They only differ on matters of*
> *Creation, sin, heaven, hell, God and salvation. . . .*

---

[17] Wiley Miller, *Non Sequitur* (November 7, 1999).

We believe that each man must find the truth that is right for him.
Reality will adapt accordingly.
The universe will readjust.
History will alter.
We believe that there is no absolute truth
Excepting the truth that there is no absolute truth.

We believe in the rejection of creeds.[18]

Don't miss the irony of Turner's closing line. As it turns out, anyone who believes in the rejection of creeds has a creed all the same.

A second major problem with postmodernism and its relativistic way of thinking is an ethical problem. If there are no absolute truths, then there can be no moral absolutes either. Who are we to judge someone else? We have no right to claim that we know the truth about what is right and what is wrong. Thus postmodernism is amoral. It says that morality, like truth itself, is a matter of personal choice. When people say that something is right or wrong, therefore, all they are really saying is that they like it or don't like it. There is no ultimate basis for morality. Greg Koukl comments: "If you believe that morality is a matter of personal definition, then you surrender the possibility of making any moral judgments on anyone else's actions ever again, no matter how offensive to your intuitive sense of right or wrong. You can express your emotions, tastes, and personal preferences, but you can't say others are wrong."[19]

If there are no ethical absolutes—no transcendent moral standards—then either you will impose your desires on me, or I will impose my desires on you, and the door is open to unspeakable cruelty. Is there a clearer example of this than Pontius Pilate? Knowing

---

[18] Steve Turner, "Creed," in *Up to Date* (London: Hodder and Stoughton, 1985), 138–39.
[19] Greg Koukl, *Solid Ground* (September–October 1998).

full well that Jesus was innocent of all accusation, the governor nevertheless committed the supreme wickedness of condemning him to the cross. He tried to wash his hands of the whole thing, of course, but the blood was still on his hands.

If we deny the claims of truth, as Pilate did, then we will believe that we can do whatever suits us. We will be like the young man who said, "I believe that everybody should just be able to do whatever they want to do." Without any moral absolutes, anything goes. And this is what we are seeing in our society. According to the pro-choice ethic of postmodern thought, deciding to kill an unborn child or an old person or a disabled person is a matter of personal preference. No one has the right to say that this is absolutely wrong. Anyone who does say this is only voicing a personal opinion. But what about oppression and injustice? What about the abuse of a child? What about the sexual violation of a defenseless woman? Are these things right for some people and wrong for others? Are they not evil in themselves, always, and for everyone? And do we not want a worldview that gives us an absolute basis for saying so?

True Truth from the God of Truth

Christianity offers a consistent worldview that is able to distinguish good from evil because it can also discriminate between truth and falsehood. It is a religion of true truth from beginning to end. So when the foundations are destroyed, the Christian can believe in a true God, who has revealed a true Word, which tells us a true story and teaches us a true theology about a true Savior, whom we know by a true Spirit, and who calls us to lead a life of true love.

It all begins with the true God. This is the place where we always start: with God himself. This was part of the genius of the Protestant Reformers: they always began with what they knew to be true about the triune God, and then worked their way up from there, as Calvin did when he began his famous *Institutes* by writing about "The Knowledge of God the Creator."[20] This is where we must always begin when we talk about truth, because without God we have no transcendent basis for truth or the knowledge of truth.

The Bible everywhere insists that there is a God, and that he is true. Truth is his very essence. It is one of the things that makes him to be God. There is no falsehood in his eternal mind, no contradiction in his essential character. The Bible therefore calls him "the true God" (2 Chron. 15:3), "the only true God" (John 17:3), and "the God of truth" (Isa. 65:16). It says that over against all the false gods that people make for themselves, "the living and true God" (1 Thess. 1:9) is the "Sovereign Lord, holy and true" (Rev. 6:10).

Not only is God true in the essence of his eternal being, but he is also true in what he does. When the Scripture speaks of God's work in the world, it often describes that work in terms of truth. "Just and true" are God's ways (Rev. 15:3), the Scripture says, "true and just" are his judgments (Rev. 16:7; 19:2). All his "commandments are true" (Ps. 119:151).

If someone asks what the truth is, as Pilate did, the answer is that the truth is God himself, *and* what God knows to be true—whether about the past, the present, or what to us is future. The truth is reality as God knows it. Our perspective is inevitably tainted by falsehood. But God remains true, and therefore, at a time when truth is fragmented into a million perspectives and thereby destroyed, there remains a vantage point from which the truth may be seen to be true. God doesn't have a point of view; he has a complete view.[21] And his view of things reflects the truth of his own being, which is the basis for all truth. The truth is what it is because God is who he is.

We also believe this: God has revealed a true Word. David

---

[20] John Calvin, *Institutes of the Christian Religion*, trans. Ford Lewis Battles, 2 vols., Library of Christian Classics, 20–21 (Philadelphia: Westminster, 1960), I.i.1.

[21] This statement comes from Matthew Sepielli and the public testimony of faith in Jesus Christ that he gave at Philadelphia's Tenth Presbyterian Church on New Year's Eve, 2004.

prayed, "O Lord GOD, you are God, and your words are true" (2 Sam. 7:28). What was true of David's prayer life is true of our theology: our doctrine of God governs our doctrine of the Word of God. We believe that the true God has spoken a true Word in the Scriptures of the Old and New Testaments. When the Bible says, "Thus saith the Lord," we believe that there is a Lord, that he has said something, and that it is so.

We believe this because God's Word makes sense of our lives like nothing else. We believe it speaks to us with power, convincing our hearts that it is the very Word of God. And we believe it because it is the testimony that the Bible gives concerning itself. These are "the true words of God" (Rev. 19:9), the Scripture says; "these words are trustworthy and true" (Rev. 21:5; 22:6). Or as Jesus said, very simply, "Your word is truth" (John 17:17).

The Protestant Reformers were committed to *sola Scriptura*— the belief that the Scripture alone is our only ultimate authority for faith and practice. We live at a time when many people resist the idea that anything or anyone else ought to have authority over them. But like the Reformers, we believe that God has spoken. And because it is *God* who has spoken, his word has authority over us. If God had not spoken, we would not and could not have any access to absolute truth. We would not have the interpreting word that makes sense of our world. It is only because God has spoken that we have knowledge of the truth. The truth is one because the one true God has given us one inerrant and infallible Word.

True Story, True Interpretation

This true Word tells us a true story—the one true story of salvation. Earlier we identified postmodernism as a revolt against the metanarrative. There is no one grand story to make sense of all there is; there are only the little stories that people tell from their own perspective.

What then is Christianity? It is the metanarrative of all metanarratives. The Bible tells us one grand story from beginning to end. It is a story that begins in eternity past, with God purposing to choose a people for himself. It is a story that tells us about the beginning of our world, when God made the universe for his glory. It is a story that tells about the tragedy of our depravity, how we fell from our high created goodness into sin and misery. But the story turns out to be a comedy, not a tragedy, because God himself comes to rescue us. This is the heart of the story: that the Son of God became a man, that he paid the price of our sin by dying on the cross, suffering under Pontius Pilate, and that he was raised from the dead with the power of eternal life. That's not the end of the story, though, because right now God is working in the world to bring his people to himself, and one day soon his Son will come again to make a new heaven and a new earth.

We have a name for this metanarrative, this story of all stories: we call it the gospel. And the best thing about it is that it is all true, every word of it. This is "the word of truth," writes the apostle Paul, "the gospel of your salvation" (Eph. 1:13; cf. Gal. 2:5; Col. 1:5).

Understand that this true gospel story is normative. In other words, it makes a claim on us; it governs our lives. This needs to be said because today some church leaders are using stories in ways that threaten to undermine the authority of God's Word. Today many so-called post-conservative evangelical Christians are enamored of what they call narrative theology. These leaders rightly perceive that stories are an ideal vehicle for reaching the emerging generation. However, one of the things they like best about stories—including Bible stories—is their ambiguity.

One leader in the emerging church has said that when it comes to theology, "clarity is overrated, and shock, obscurity, playfulness, and intrigue often stimulate more thought than clarity."[22] Clarity

---

[22] Brian D. McLaren, author of *A Generous Orthodoxy* (Grand Rapids, MI: Zondervan, 2004), as quoted in a network newsletter for the emerging church.

may or may not stimulate more thought, but in any case, God wants to do something more than get us thinking: he wants to give us saving knowledge of the truth. He wants to have—as the Alliance of Confessing Evangelicals says in its mission statement—"clarity and conviction about the truths of the gospel." To that end, God has given us a story that provides a clear perspective on reality. This makes the Bible fundamentally different from all other stories. The gospel is not merely another metanarrative; it is *the* true metanarrative. It is the true story that God tells about what God has done so that we will know what to believe and how to behave. It is characteristic of sound theology that it stays true to the gospel narrative, telling God's story the way God wants it to be told.

We need to add something to this, because the Bible gives us more than the true story; it also gives us the true interpretation of the true story. The Bible as a whole is structured as a story. However, story is not the only kind of literature we find in the Bible. The Bible is an anthology of stories, poems, letters, treatises, genealogies, historical records, and apocalyptic visions of the future. In addition to telling us a true story, these forms of biblical literature teach us a true theology.

This needs to be emphasized because postmodernism is strongly opposed to propositional truth, and this attitude is having a harmful effect on evangelical theology. Today we often hear that creeds and confessions are outmoded. Rather than defining the Christian faith in terms of its theology, people say, we need to define it in terms of its story. Doctrine is de-emphasized, especially if it deals with difficult or intolerant subjects like sin, judgment, wrath, and atonement through a sacrifice of blood. Many people—including many preachers—would rather not discuss these or any other doctrines. To quote again from one of the gurus of the emerging church, "the gospel is not primarily informational but relational."[23]

---

[23] Brian D. McLaren, as quoted in a network newsletter for the emerging church.

But of course this is a false dichotomy. The gospel *is* relational because it establishes a reconciled relationship between fallen sinners and a holy God. However, the gospel cannot be relational unless it also gives us true information about God and about us—about Jesus, the cross, and the empty tomb. The gospel is information that brings transformation.

In order for the gospel to have this transforming effect, it needs to be explained. Stories are not self-interpreting. Therefore, God has given us a true theology to explain the gospel story. This is why God's Word is written the way that it is. The gospels are followed by long doctrinal letters that teach basic truths about God and his salvation, and it is characteristic of these letters to give us truth in the form of propositions. As Luther said, "There is no Christianity where there are no assertions."[24] So the Bible asserts, for example, that God chose us in Christ before the foundation of the world (Eph. 1:4). Or it says we have been saved by grace through faith (Eph. 2:8). The Bible is full of theological propositions—unchanging truths of the Christian faith.

Not only does the Bible make such affirmations, but it also makes corresponding denials. If certain things are true, then certain other things are false. To paraphrase Luther, there is no Christianity where there is no antithesis. The Bible is constantly discriminating between truth and falsehood, especially in relationship to the gospel. For example, when the Bible says that we are saved by grace through faith, it also says that we are *not* saved by works, so that no one can boast. Or when it speaks of election, it says that the sovereign choice of God does *not* depend on anything that we do, but only on the mercy of God (Rom. 9:16). The truth of any one doctrine excludes everything that is contrary to it. As far as the Bible is concerned, truth is not merely a point of view; it is something to believe and to

---

[24] Martin Luther, quoted in Bruce Milne, *Know the Truth*, rev. ed. (Downers Grove, IL: InterVarsity, 1998), 234.

live over against what is false. "We must act upon, witness, and preach this fact," wrote Francis Schaeffer, that "what is contrary to God's revealed propositional truth is not true."[25]

This means that the truth always forces us to make a choice. We cannot be both for and against the truth. We have to choose. If we are not for the truth—the truth that God has revealed in the story *and* the theology of his Word—then we are against it.

True Savior, True Spirit

This was the position in which Pontius Pilate found himself on the night that Jesus was betrayed. Remember Pilate's dilemma? He wanted to defer his decision by casting doubt on the very idea that anyone can ever really know the truth. But Jesus demanded Pilate to make a choice: "For this purpose I was born and for this purpose I have come into the world—to bear witness to the truth. Everyone who is of the truth listens to my voice" (John 18:37).

Here Jesus defines his mission to the world in terms of truth. Why did the Son of God come into the world? To tell us the truth. Jesus Christ is the true Savior, who was and is the true Word of God, incarnate. Elsewhere John describes Jesus as the true light (John 1:9), the true bread (John 6:32), and the true vine (John 15:1). He calls Jesus "the faithful and true witness" (Rev. 3:14). He says that Jesus came from the Father "full of grace and truth" (John 1:14). He says, "we know that the Son of God has come . . . so that we may know him who is true; and we are in him who is true, in his Son Jesus Christ. He is the true God and eternal life" (1 John 5:20). Or as Jesus simply said, "I am . . . the truth" (John 14:6).

If Jesus is true, then when people attack his claim to be the one and only true Savior of the world—as some Christians do today in the name of religious pluralism—they are attacking the very foun-

---

[25] Francis A. Schaeffer, *The Church at the End of the Twentieth Century*, in *Works*, 5 vols. (Wheaton, IL: Crossway, 1982), 4:32.

dations of truth. Jesus is not *a* truth; he is *the* truth. It is in him that "all things hold together" (Col. 1:17), including the truthfulness of truth. All truth is God's truth, and this truth finds its unifying center in Jesus Christ.

Since Jesus is true, everything he has done, or is doing, or will do is absolutely true. He was true in his work of creation and in the governance of his providence. He was true in the work of salvation: true in teaching the will of God, true in obeying the law, true in atoning for sin, and true in rising to resurrection life. He is true in his present dominion over heaven and earth. And he will be true in keeping all his promises, true in the coming of his kingdom, and true in his everlasting glory. Jesus Christ is the truth itself, in his very person, and therefore he is true in everything he does, from eternity past to eternity future. In the words of Wheaton College President Duane Litfin, "Because God's reality is unified and coherent, centered as it is on the person of Christ, all truthful apprehensions of that reality, or truthful expressions of those apprehensions, will cohere and contribute to an integrated, unified, Christ-centered vision of all things."[26]

How wonderful it is that in Christ we have truth in person! Consider the plight of an elderly couple that was puzzling over the instructions for their first microwave oven. Finally, in total exasperation the old woman said, "If only my son had come along with the instructions." This is what God has done for us in Christ: he has sent his Son along with the instructions, so that we can have personal saving knowledge of him.

If Jesus is true, then it follows that whatever decision we make about Jesus is a decision either for or against the truth. The true God has told us a true story to teach us a true theology about a true Savior. If we are for the truth, then we will listen to him. But if we do not listen to Jesus, then we are really against the truth, as Pilate was, and God will judge us for our falsehood.

---

[26] Duane Litfin, *Conceiving the Christian College* (Grand Rapids: Eerdmans, 2004), 94.

How do we know that all this is true? How can we know the truth that will save us and set us free? This is an important question, because not everyone who reads the true Word, or hears the true gospel story, or listens to true theology, or is introduced to the true Savior believes that these things are true. So how can we know the truth for sure? How can we get beyond the question that Pilate asked, and that some people keep asking over and over again without ever really getting the right answer: What is truth?

The answer is that God has sent his Holy Spirit to teach us the truth. Everything we have said about the truth of God and the truth of God the Son is also true of God the Holy Spirit, who is called "the Spirit of truth" (John 14:17). The Third Person of the Trinity fully shares in the divine attribute of truth. "The Spirit is the truth," wrote the Apostle John (1 John 5:6). Therefore, as Christians we have a fully Trinitarian understanding of the truth.

The true Spirit is the Person of the Trinity who wrote the true Word that we read in the Scriptures of the Old and New Testaments. It is the Spirit who inspired the Bible, the Spirit who told the true story of salvation that we read in the gospels, and the Spirit who teaches us the true theology of the Bible. As John Calvin said in one of his letters on reforming the church, "The Holy Spirit is a faithful and unerring witness to our doctrine. We know, I say, that it is the eternal truth of God that we preach."[27]

Now the Father and the Son have sent that very same Spirit into the world to teach people the truth (see John 15:26; 16:13). This is the source of our confidence in teaching the truth. As Calvin went on to say: "We are indeed desirous, as we ought to be, that our ministry may prove salutary to the world; but to give it this effect belongs to [the Spirit of] God, not to us."[28]

This means that our knowledge of God's truth is not subjective,

---

[27] John Calvin, *The Necessity of Reforming the Church*, trans. and ed. Henry Beveridge (Dallas, TX: Heritage, 1995).
[28] Ibid.

in the sense that it comes from something inside us. If it were merely subjective, how could we claim to know the absolute truth? But our knowledge of the truth is *not* subjective; it is objective. It comes from someone outside of us, namely, from the Holy Spirit of God. The same God who is the truth and does the truth comes to help us know the truth. Therefore, we have personal knowledge of the truth through the assuring presence of God himself in our minds and hearts. Like everything else in the Christian life, knowledge of the truth only comes by grace. We know the absolute truth, not because of who we are, but because of who God is.

A Life of True Love

We believe that the true God has revealed a true Word, which tells us a true story and teaches us true theology about a true Savior, whom we know by the Spirit of truth. But what is the point of all this? Is it simply so that we will know the truth? No, it is so that we may *live* the truth to the glory of God.

The Bible says many things about standing with Jesus on the side of truth. It tells us to worship in truth (John 4:24), rejoice in truth (1 Cor. 13:6), obey the truth (1 Pet. 1:22), be established in the truth (2 Pet. 1:12), walk in the truth (e.g., Eph. 5:8–9; 2 John 4), do the truth (1 John 3:18), and speak the truth in our hearts (Ps. 15:2). Truth is not a theory for the believer in Christ; it is a way of life. But of all the things that we could say about living as people of the truth, let us never forget the crucial importance of "speaking the truth in love" (Eph. 4:15).

This needs to be emphasized because Christians who say they love the truth do not always truly love. And unless we love, few people will listen to the claims we make about the truth. Why is it that our culture seems increasingly hostile to absolute truth in general and to the truth of Christianity in particular? Is it because people have a problem with the truth itself? Yes, they certainly do. As the Scripture says, "They refused to love the truth and so be saved"

(2 Thess. 2:10). But could it also be that they reject the truth because our lack of love makes it unattractive?

When some people hear the words "absolute truth" they immediately think of someone who is proud and self-righteous, someone who wants to tell everyone else what to think, but doesn't want to listen. Is that a total misconception, or is there some truth to it? And wouldn't we be more effective in our witness if we had *both* a stronger commitment to theological truth *and* a more obvious commitment to sacrificial love?

The English apologist G. K. Chesterton once commented that we are living in a time when people are timid about the truth but confident about themselves. His point was that as followers of Jesus Christ, we are called to have exactly the opposite attitude. We should be confident about the truth, and therefore bold in our defense of God, his Word, and the gospel of Jesus Christ. But we, of all people, should know better than to be confident about ourselves! We should know how sinful we are, how prone we are to misunderstand things and thus to fail in living out the truth. We should know what a mystery it is that God's infallible, inerrant truth has been entrusted to fallen, fallible people. We should know that our own grasp of the absolute truth is far from absolute.

We should also know that with knowledge of the truth comes the high call to serve others in sacrificial love. We only live the truth when we live like the Christ who is the truth. This means being at the forefront of mercy ministry in our communities. It means empathizing with fallen and broken sinners in the struggle of their bondage with sin. It means reaching out in friendship to people whose values we reject and whose lifestyle we may find repellent. It means setting aside our own agenda so that we can be like Christ to people in need. Then, perhaps, after we have lived in love, people will give us the opportunity to tell them what we know about the truth.

Who is sufficient for these things? Who is able to defend the truth of God's Word while at the same time living out the love of the gospel?

We can only do this through the saving work of Jesus Christ and the transforming work of his Spirit. In our own strength we might be able to defend the truth without living in love, or to live in love without defending truth, but we could not have both together. Without the love of God, inevitably we become harsh, judgmental, and legalistic in our defense of the truth; without the truth of God our love becomes an excuse for theological compromise. Sadly, this is what we usually see in the church: truth without love, or love without truth. But on those rare occasions when we do find love and truth together we know that this can only be a gracious work of the one true God,[29] who will use the union of love and truth to save dying sinners. The best apologetic for the absolute truth of the gospel of Jesus Christ is a community that lives by his love.

How will we answer the challenge that Jesus gave to Pilate? Are we on the side of truth? If we are, then by the grace of God we will live out the truth we believe in the way that we behave.

---

[29] Francis Schaeffer makes a similar point about love and purity in *The Church at the End of the Twentieth Century*, in *Works*, 4:98.

5

One People

J. LIGON DUNCAN III

But you are a chosen race, a royal priesthood, a holy nation, a people for God's own possession, that you may proclaim the excellencies of Him who has called you out of darkness into His marvelous light; for you once were not a people, but now you are the people of God; you had not received mercy, but now you have received mercy.

1 PETER 2:9–10[1]

Before examining what Peter has to say about the people of God, several introductory remarks are in order. We can begin by saying that the Bible's teaching about the church is grounded in the doctrine of union with Jesus Christ. From his eternal counsels to his work of creation, including the very first announcements of grace to Adam and Eve after their fall (see Gen. 3:15), God has been working out in history his redeeming plan that will culminate in one people from every tribe, tongue, and nation.

We know that we who are united to Christ are saved and are the beneficiaries of all the blessings that flow from his person and work on our behalf in redemption. But there is also a corollary truth: that when you are united to Jesus Christ—when by the work

---

[1] Unless otherwise noted, Scripture references in this chapter are taken from the *New American Standard Version* of the Bible (NASB).

of the Holy Spirit you trust in Jesus Christ alone for salvation as he is offered in the gospel, and you are united to him by the Spirit through faith—you are also united to all others who are united to Jesus Christ. We are united to Christ our head, but we are also united to all others who are united to Jesus Christ. We are one body. Paul says that over and over in the New Testament. God has not saved us to be *Lone Rangers*. He saved us into a body; we need one another.

One of the reasons I love going to conferences like PCRT, the genesis of the material in this chapter, is the opportunity to fellowship with the people of God and to sit under the teaching of brothers who can preach God's word far more effectively than I can, being ministered to by them. I love reveling in the glorious truth of Scripture, in these glorious redemptive realities which have been laid open for us in the Word of God revealed, and enjoying the strengthening of God's people.

But if there is anything that I enjoy more than that, it is being with my own congregation—the local church to which God has called me to be accountable to shepherd and feed—that body of people who know me in all my weaknesses, all my sins, all my mistakes, and all my failings. I enjoy being there to minister to them in their weaknesses and to share with them as we help one another. This is how God intended it to be. He did not call us to be off on our own. He called us into a body. The doctrine of union with Christ is one of the great realities that grounds our understanding of what it means to be the people of God, because when we are united to Christ, we are united with all those who are united to Jesus Christ.

But there is a second great reality as well, and that is the Bible's teaching on the church, which is grounded in the doctrine of the covenant of grace. When God called Abraham out of paganism, out of the Ur of the Chaldees, and into his covenant of grace, he called him into a family. His purpose was not simply to have a personal relationship with Abraham, though certainly that was one of the great things entailed in Abraham's being brought into this saving relationship to God. But his purpose was to make of Abraham a people and a nation that was to be a blessing to all the nations of the earth. God's purpose was corporate.

We see how this worked out many, many years later, long after the death of Abraham. God heard the cries of his people in Egypt, and he responded to those cries and inaugurated a work of redemption that would lead to his judgment against Pharaoh in Egypt. Israel would cross the Red Sea on dry land and continue on to Sinai where they would be made to be a great people. What does Exodus 2:24–25 say that God was doing when he made a great people, a great nation, out of the descendants of Abraham and consecrated and inaugurated them as a holy people to his name at Mount Sinai? He was simply fulfilling the promises that he had made to Abraham. When the cries of the people of God in Egypt came up to his ears, he remembered the promise, the covenant that he had made with Abraham.

So the doctrine of the church, our understanding of it, is grounded in the doctrine of the covenant of grace. God's work of grace in his covenant of grace creates the people of God, the church.

It is also true that the church is not peripheral or optional. We live in a day and time when many Christians believe that the local church is not essential to the Christian life. They may or may not belong to a body of believers. They may or may not be accountable to brothers and sisters in Christ. They may or may not be under the authority of God's Bible-believing, Christ-exalting, gospel-preaching shepherd. It may or may not matter, they think. But as Matthew Henry reminds us, when we take God for our God, we take his people for our own. From Augustine and Calvin, 1500 and 500 years ago respectively, we are reminded that we cannot have God for our Father if we refuse to have the church for our mother. That is not

Roman Catholic teaching; it is biblical teaching. God has ordained that when we are united to Christ we are saved into his body. So we need one another. And in a land and time that is assailed by individualism, narcissism, and a spirit that dislikes authority and accountability, we need to hear the Bible's teaching on the church, because God has saved us into this one body.

Finally, by way of introduction, it is instructive to remember that the early church fathers spoke of the unity of believers as one of the four ancient marks of the church. In the Protestant and Reformed tradition, however, we often list three: the right preaching of the word, the right administration of the sacraments, and the right administration of discipline in the church. And that is appropriate. Those are biblical emphases. But the men and women of the earliest church would surely have given a different list—it is one, holy, catholic, apostolic church. *Unum, sanctum, catholicam, apostolicam.*

The oneness of the church (*unum*) is a very important emphasis in the teaching of our great Reformation heritage. God has not created two peoples—a Plan A group and a Plan B group, a first class and a second class, literal, physical descendants of Israel and a group of leftovers, an afterthought of the great parenthesis—but one people in all ages, in all generations, in all times, and in all places. The Christian church is not an afterthought. It is the intended culmination of God's plan, inaugurated at the very beginning of the ages.

And we are united, even now in the Christian church, with all those who are united to Christ, to all those who have gone on before, tracing fifty generations back to the time of Christ and fifty more generations back to the time of Abraham, and all the way back to the time of Adam. Those are our people. And when we gather on the Lord's Day and lift up our voices in praise, our voices are mingled with their voices above, as they stand before the throne ever singing "Holy, holy, holy" and "Worthy is the lamb who was slain from the foundation of the world." Our voices are mingled with their voices and with the voices of God's people all around the world. Everywhere Jesus alone is trusted for salvation as he is offered in the gospel, there our brothers and sisters are, and we are united with them. Those are our people. So this glorious truth of one people of God flows out of the glorious truth of one God, one way of salvation, one Savior, and one truth.

1 Peter 2:9–10 Echoing the Old Testament

> But you are a chosen race, a royal priesthood, a holy nation, a people for God's own possession, that you may proclaim the excellencies of Him who has called you out of darkness into His marvelous light; for you once were not a people, but now you are the people of God; you had not received mercy, but now you have received mercy (1 Pet. 2:9–10).

Peter is here addressing a people who were literally resident aliens. They lived in Asia Minor, but they were considered to be strangers by their neighbors because of their allegiance to the Lord Jesus Christ. They were Jews and Gentiles, but they were marginal, second-class citizens in the eyes of their peers and their neighbors. They did not know it, but in a matter of months, the recipients of Peter's letter were going to undergo persecution under the Emperor Nero. So the apostle Peter is speaking to them in this epistle, encouraging them to live the Christian life and to take great confidence, consolation, and comfort from the grand truths of salvation and of the body of Christ, the church.

Calvin says in his commentary on Peter's letter that the main object of this letter, the epistle, is to call believers to rise above the world in order that we may be prepared and encouraged for the battle of spiritual warfare; for this purpose the knowledge of God's benefits is of great help, for when we appreciate their value all other things will become worthless by comparison. When we consider all that Christ and his blessings are to us, everything without him will seem as loss.

Peter is setting before us the glorious blessings and realities of salvation in Jesus Christ in order to encourage us. When Peter says these words to Christians—Jewish and Gentile Christians gathered in this congregation or group of congregations in Asia Minor—he is saying to them something that they already know about the people of God from their Bibles, because in the Old Testament God says this:

> You yourselves have seen what I did to the Egyptians, and how I bore you on eagles' wings, and brought you to Myself. Now then, if you will indeed obey My voice and keep My covenant, then you shall be My own possession among all the peoples, for all the earth is Mine; and you shall be to Me a kingdom of priests and a holy nation. (Ex. 19:4–6)

We also find, in Moses' sermon to the people of God:

> You are a holy people to the LORD your God. The LORD your God has chosen you to be a people for His own possession out of all the peoples who are on the face of the earth. The LORD did not set his love on you nor choose you because you were more in number than any of the peoples, for you were the fewest of all peoples, but because the LORD loved you and kept the oath which He swore to your forefathers, the LORD brought you out by a mighty hand, and redeemed you from the house of slavery, from the hand of Pharaoh king of Egypt. (Deut. 7:6–8)

Peter is reminding us of the grand and glorious truth that God's redemptive word, God's covenant word, God's word of promise and grace, has brought into being one people, one family, one household, one church (1 Pet. 2:9–10). He is reminding us that in the redeeming work of Jesus Christ, he has created a new people. They are a new creation. He is reminding us that in the redeeming work of Jesus Christ, the promise of the ages, the promise of the covenant of grace, the promise of the word of God to Abraham has come into fulfillment: "You will be My people and I will be your God."

Peter is employing this teaching on the people of God in the service of exhorting God's people to live lives that bear witness to God in this world and that are in accordance with God's own holiness. The context of 1 Peter 2 is instructive. He begins this chapter by calling on them to lay aside certain behaviors. Then after speaking to them about what they are (a chosen race, a royal priesthood, a holy nation, a people for God's own possession), he says in verse 11, "Beloved, I urge you as aliens and strangers to abstain from fleshly lusts." So once again, the realization of who they are will lead them to abstain from certain things. However, they are not simply to lay aside certain things, but also to pick up and to live in a certain way: "Keep your behavior excellent among the Gentiles, so that in the thing which they slander you as evildoers, they may on account of your good deeds, as they observe them, glorify God in the day of visitation" (v. 12). Peter is deploying his teaching about who we are in Christ as the church, as the people of God, in the service of this exhortation to Christian living. Peter is saying to these Christians, to these churches, *Be who you are. Be who God has made you to be in Jesus Christ. Live out the reality of what God has made you to be in Jesus Christ.*

John Owen was one of the most brilliant men ever to live. He was leader of the prestigious school of divinity at Oxford and author of twenty-four volumes of the most exalted theology. And yet with that capacious mind and extensive writing, he once observed that the work of the pastor boils down to just two things—two components to pastoral ministry, two pastoral problems that must be faced. The first problem we face is to make those who are not united to Jesus Christ to realize that they are not united to him. The second great task is to make those who are united to

Jesus Christ to realize that they are united to Jesus Christ.[2] Isn't that glorious? Isn't that beautiful in its simplicity? You see, that is exactly what Peter is doing here. He is calling those who are united to Jesus Christ, saying, *Would you please realize that you are united to Jesus Christ? Would you realize what that means for you, and would you live your life in accordance with that glorious reality?*

Peter is trying to press home four points from these great realities that flow from our union and communion with Jesus Christ.

God's People by Discrimination

The first point is found in the phrase "You are a chosen race." The church is God's people by discrimination. God has chosen you out of the world to be his one people, distinguished from the world by God's electing choice. You have been made one family distinct in this world because God has set his love on you and adopted you into his family. God has chosen you by his divine and unconditional election to be his family.

Peter is saying to these Christians, *What makes you one people is not your shared ethnicity, because you are made up of Jew and Gentile. What makes you one people is not your shared culture, because you have come from every tribe and tongue and people and nation. It is not your shared geography, because you are spread to the far-flung corners of this world. It is not your shared genealogy, unless you take it all the way back to Adam. What makes you one people is not shared chronology, but God's divine choice of you and your faith union with Jesus Christ. That's what makes you one. You are united to Christ by his divine and electing choice and call.* You see how incredibly encouraging this would be to these people who are on the verge of persecution and who are

---

[2] Sinclair B. Ferguson, *John Owen on the Christian Life* (Edinburgh: Banner of Truth, 2001), 127.

already accredited as second-class citizens and peripheral in their own culture.

Peter is saying that the church is God's chosen people, adopted deliberately by discrimination into his family. That is the reality that we sing about in an old, old hymn. Perhaps you have never heard it. If you haven't, you need to add this one into your hymn vocabulary. It goes like this:

> *I sought the Lord, and afterward I knew he moved my soul*
> *   to seek him, seeking me;*
> *It was not I that found, O Savior true; no, I was found of thee.*
> *Thou didst reach forth thy hand and mine enfold; I walked*
> *   and sank not on the storm-vexed sea—*
> *'Twas not so much that I on thee took hold, as thou,*
> *   dear Lord, on me.*
> *I find, I walk, I love, but O the whole of love is but my answer,*
> *   Lord, to thee;*
> *For thou wert long beforehand with my soul,*
> *   always thou lovedst me.*[3]

What was it that the great apostle John said, in the year just before his death? "We love, because He first loved us" (1 John 4:19). Our faith is a response to his grace. Our love is a response to his love. We are his chosen people. Peter is saying you are God's people not because you have been hoisted onto him or because you have chosen him. You are God's people because he has chosen you.

Professor Willie Ruff of the Yale School of Music is a very famous ethnomusicologist. He studies the history of various aspects of American jazz. He has put forward a very interesting theory which has by no means been accepted by all students of the history of music. He theorizes that the roots of jazz are not to be found in Africa but in the West Highlands of Scotland. He has done some

---

[3] Author unknown.

very interesting experiments to try to demonstrate this. But one of his most interesting experiments was performed while he was traveling among some Baptist churches in North Alabama. He heard in those predominately African-American Baptist congregations a very strange type of singing—*line singing*—where someone sings out a hymn stanza—a line—and then the congregation sings out that same line behind him, back and forth all the way through the song. Ruff wondered where this distinctive style of music came from until later when he was visiting Scotland. He met a man who worshiped in a psalm-singing congregation. Ruff spoke with him about line singing, and the man said, "Well, you know, that is exactly how they sing in the West Highlands of Scotland."

Professor Ruff said, "I've got to hear this." So he was taken to the West Highlands of Scotland and heard Gaelic psalm singers "lining out a line" and the congregation responding. He returned and gathered some ladies from the congregations in North Alabama, took them to the Isle of Lewis in Scotland, and sat them down in the middle of these Presbyterian congregations. When they heard the line singing, one of the ladies turned to a Presbyterian minister with tears in her eyes and said, "These are my people." I don't know if she was thinking particularly about the way they sang or maybe she felt a spiritual connection with them. But the story illustrates what Peter was saying in his epistle. You have been chosen by God to be his people.

This doctrine of election disturbs a lot of fine people. They do not think it is fair. They believe it makes God's people prideful. But in fact, the doctrine of God's choosing does the exact opposite—it humbles us. If you want to complain about a doctrine being unfair, then complain about the reward of heaven by grace. If ever there was an unfair doctrine, it is that. Hell, on the other hand, is the fairest doctrine in the world. Heaven by grace—that is purely discrimination. There is nothing more humbling than the realization that you are saved by grace alone because of absolutely nothing you have done or will do. There is no one who has really embraced the doctrine of God's sovereign choosing and is proud of that fact. You can be a Reformed Calvinist, or you can be prideful, but you can't be both. This truth humbles us to the dust.

I love the way that Isaac Watts expressed it in his glorious hymn *How Sweet and Awesome Is the Place*, another hymn you need in your vocabulary if it is not there already.

> *How sweet and awesome is the place with Christ within the doors,*
> *While everlasting love displays the choicest of her stores.*
>
> *While all our hearts and all our songs join to admire the feast,*
> *Each of us cries, with thankful tongue, "Lord, why was I a guest?"*
>
> *"Why was I made to hear your voice, and enter while there's room,*
> *When thousands make a wretched choice, and rather starve than come?"*
>
> *'Twas the same love that spread the feast that sweetly drew us in;*
> *Else we had still refused to taste, and perished in our sin.*

I love this hymn because it doesn't stop there. The glorious exaltation of the electing grace of God goes on. The hymnwriter has realized the choosing grace of God, and what has such recognition done? It has humbled him. He sees that he doesn't deserve it. That is precisely the reaction that God's grace brings, because his grace shines a spotlight on his Son. What God requires, he provides in him. The Son earned that which you cannot. He delivers that which you cannot. He secures that which you cannot. And so the hymn asks, "Why was I a guest?" That is the right humble response to this grace. The hymn continues:

> *Pity the nations, O our God, constrain the earth to come;*
> *Send your victorious Word abroad, and bring the strangers home.*

Isn't that the most beautiful way to think about missions? "Bring the strangers home." We want every tribe and people and tongue and nation to come home. We want the strangers to come home, the prodigals to come home. The final stanza takes us further:

We long to see your churches full, that all the chosen race
May, with one voice and heart and soul, sing your redeeming
grace.[4]

That is the response of a person who really understands the doctrines of grace. He is humbled and he wants to see men and women and boys and girls from every tribe and tongue and people and nation come to a saving knowledge of Jesus Christ. He knows that it will happen because God has chosen a multitude that no man can number from every tribe and tongue and people and nation to be savingly united with Jesus Christ, and it will be our glorious privilege to go out and call them to saving faith in Jesus Christ. We know that word will not return void. You see, believing the doctrines of grace does not discourage us from evangelism; it impels us to it.

God's People for Service

We find our second point in Peter's phrase "a royal priesthood" (v. 9). It is a mixing of metaphors: a *royal priesthood*, or *kingly priests*, or a *priestly kingdom*. What does that mean? It means that God's people are a serving people. The church is God's by discrimination, and the church is God's for service because God's one people are a serving people.

An old Anglican commentator made a beautiful observation on this text. When meditating on what it means to be a royal priest-

---

[4] Isaac Watts, "How Sweet and Awesome Is the Place," 1707.

hood he said, "What is the essence of the role of a king and of a priest? They lived for others." We typically do not think of kings in that role, do we? We think of kings living for themselves. But a real king, a good king, lives for others. His concern, when he puts his boots on and his feet in the stirrups, is for his people. He lives for his people—their well being, their protection, the securement of their enjoyment of domestic happiness. His desire is for his people. He serves them with every breath of his life. He longs for their blessing. That is the picture of the good king in the Old Testament, David, who sought to serve his people. The greatest king of all, the Lord Jesus Christ, is the ultimate example of the good king. He laid down his life for his people.

Service is the essence of a king and, of course, by very nature service is the essence of priesthood. What does a priest do but serve the people of God as God's representative to his people and as the people's representative to God? The whole of the priest's life is one of service. So when Peter says, *Now, one people of God, let me remind you of who you are. You are not only chosen by God, but you are chosen by God to be royal priests*, what does he mean? Peter is referring to the fact that God's people have been chosen by God to be royal, serving priests. Our saving election transforms us from servants of self, the world, the flesh, and the devil, into servants of the Lord, free to serve the people of God and to do God's bidding. That great twentieth-century theologian Bob Dylan put it this way: "You may serve the devil or you may serve the Lord. But you've all got to serve somebody."[5]

Peter is saying, *Christians, God has called you out of bondage to sin and self and Satan into the glorious freedom of the sons of God so that you can serve because the great freedom of the Christian life is experienced when we deny ourselves and we take*

---

[5] Bob Dylan, "Gotta Serve Somebody," 1979.

up our cross and we die daily and we give ourselves away in service to one another.

Our Arminian friends (those who do not embrace the doctrines of grace taught in Scripture) will often draw a distinction. They will say that we are not elected to salvation but are elected to serve. We choose, thereby gaining salvation, and God elects that all those who have chosen him will serve. Now those of us who embrace the doctrines of grace do not disagree that we are chosen to serve. Peter says as much here in his epistle. The apostle Paul writes it in Ephesians 1 and 2. We can find it all over the New Testament. But we cannot separate the two; we are chosen for salvation *and* service. We are saved to serve, a point Paul makes clear:

> For by grace you have been saved through faith; and that not of yourselves, it is the gift of God; not as a result of works, and that no one should boast. For we are His workmanship, created in Christ Jesus for good works, which God prepared beforehand, so that we would walk in them. (Eph. 2:8–10)

We have been called and saved, not *by*, but *to* these good works. Joe Novenson puts it this way:

> When Abraham was called by God out of paganism into the covenant of grace, God changed him from being a guest on this planet to being a host.[6]

It was his privilege not simply to be an occupant of God's world, but now to serve God as God's representative, hosting the nations, seeking to be a blessing, seeking to serve the welfare of every nation. And that is us. We have been called to serve.

Those who would be servants must be prepared to be treated

---

[6] Joe Novenson, *God's Missionary Strategy*, sermon on Genesis 17:1–14 delivered at FPC Missions Conference, First Presbyterian Church, Jackson, MS, February 13, 2000.

like servants from time to time. Aspiring to be a servant leader and having great passion for God's people may be very noble. But service is hard. It is especially hard when the very people that you are trying to serve let you down.

One of my professors once served during a communion season in the North Highlands of Scotland and after giving his message, a little old lady approached him and said, "You know, Professor, the older I grow, the more I love the Lord's people."

"Isn't that sweet," he thought. But she wasn't finished.

"You know, Professor, the older I grow, the more I love the Lord's people and the less I trust them."

The Lord's people will hurt you. You will seek to serve the Lord's people; they will let you down. When that happens, you are being given the privilege of reflecting your Savior, because he washed the feet of disciples who abandoned him. So if you are going to be a part of this people, if you are going to be in this body, it is not about what that body is going to do for you; it is about how you are going to serve that body. The test of whether you really believe in the unity of and service to the one people of God is when you are disappointed and let down in the assembly of God's people. When the church fails you in some time of need, will you stand on your rights and say, "I deserve to be treated better than that," or will you respond as a servant? When you serve and are not acknowledged, when you serve and are not recognized, when you serve and are let down and betrayed, will you still love the Lord Jesus? Will you still serve?

That is what Peter is saying. You are a chosen people and you are a serving people.

God's People for Holiness

Peter goes on to say a third thing: *You are a holy people.* Not only are we a chosen race and a royal priesthood, but we are also a holy nation. God's church is called to holiness because God has called us to be like him; i.e., we are to be holy because he is holy. The church is called unto holiness.

Ephesians 2 shows us that we are not saved *by* holiness. If we were, we would all be going to hell. But we are saved *to* holiness; we are saved *to* good works. Peter is reminding this body of believers, and he is reminding you and me, that we are called to be holy. We are called to be the image of God—the living, breathing, walking, talking reflection of the God whom we love and serve.

In the Old Testament God made his people holy and distinct by drawing boundaries around them and separating them from the rest of the world through the ceremonial and ritual code:

> The LORD spoke again to Moses and Aaron, saying to them, "Speak to the sons of Israel, saying, 'These are the creatures which you may eat from all the animals that are on the earth. Whatever divides a hoof, thus making split hoofs, and chews the cud, among the animals, that you may eat. Nevertheless, you are not to eat of these, among those which chew the cud, or among those which divide the hoof: the camel, for though it chews cud, it does not divide the hoof, it is unclean to you. Likewise, the [rock badger], for though it chews cud, it does not divide the hoof, it is unclean to you; the rabbit also, for though it chews cud, it does not divide the hoof, it is unclean to you; and the pig, for though it divides the hoof, thus making a split hoof, it does not chew cud, it is unclean to you. You shall not eat of their flesh nor touch their carcasses; they are unclean to you.'" (Lev. 11:1–8)

Of course your response to that is *Huh? What in the world is God talking about in this chapter, with all these minute distinctions between clean and unclean animals?* Commentators offer all sorts of suggestions for why God declared some animals clean and others unclean. But the bottom line is this: it is a strategy for holiness. If you want to create a people in the world that is going to be distinct, unsullied by the religious beliefs and worldviews and moral activities of pagan nations, then what better way to create a distinct people than to create ways that prevent them from fellowshiping with those people? And what better way to prevent them from fellowshipping with those people than to prohibit the food that the pagans eat? In so doing, God's people are given a boundary that keeps them from sitting down in the homes of their pagan neighbors, sharing a meal with them, and getting to be buddies over a meal.

The food laws, at the very least, are designed to build a structure into the life of Israel so they cannot intermingle with the nations around them. There is a ritual, ceremonial holiness that is created for the people of God. But, of course, we live in the new covenant era. And those ceremonial, ritual codes are gone. Peter saw the spread of clean and unclean food come down from heaven and he heard the voice of the Lord say, "What God has cleansed, no *longer* consider unholy" (Acts 10:15). So how is the Christian to be distinct from the world? The Christian is to be *morally* distinct from the world. The Christian, by his or her behavior, is to be distinct in the world. We are to be image-bearers; we are to show by our behavior that we are followers of the living God. We are to be a holy nation.

A number of years ago a man who owned a number of large automobile dealerships in a particular part of the country came to a very famous minister and said, "You know, I want to find a way to bear witness to Christ. I would like to hand out gospel tracts to everybody who buys a car in my automobile dealership. What do you think of it, pastor?"

This pastor happened to know that the auto dealer had a reputation for unscrupulous dealings with his customers, and his integrity was not highly honored or esteemed in the eyes of the community. So the pastor said, "That is an interesting idea, but you know what would be better for you to do as a Christian? Don't cheat your customers."

He was to bear witness to the holiness of God in the way he

treated those customers as human beings made in the image of God. He was to treat them with dignity and with justice and fairness and *then* talk about Jesus. If you talk about Jesus while you live in unholiness, you make a mockery of the claims of God. And isn't that exactly what the American church is doing today? Isn't it precisely worldliness that is robbing us of our witness to the world, because we are like the world? We think like the world, we love what the world loves, and we act like the world. Is it any wonder the world doesn't listen to us? Peter is saying, brothers and sisters, we are a holy nation.

God's People as His Inheritance

Finally, Peter is saying that we are "a people for *God's* own possession" (1 Pet. 2:9). The church is God's special delight. This interesting phrase was translated in the *King James Bible* as: "a peculiar people." The term actually refers to the overtime earnings that a slave would get. If a slave in the Greco-Roman world did things outside of the sphere of his normal responsibilities for his master, whatever he earned for that activity would be called his "peculiar possession," his own particular and unique and distinct possession. It is we, the people of God, who are God's peculiar possession. We are his unique treasure. We are his possession. We are his inheritance.

There are two great themes regarding the inheritance of God in the Old and the New Testaments. One theme is the inheritance that God is going to give us. From Old to New Testament it is clear that God has made us to be joint heirs in Jesus Christ, and we will inherit with Jesus Christ that which God is preparing for us from the foundation of the world. The other theme is this: that we are God's inheritance, chosen by and for himself out of this grand work of redemption.

I want you to think hard about this for a moment. It is, of course, true that God does not need anything. God is not the debtor of anything within this created world. In that light, consider what

Peter says: though God does not need anything in this world, he has chosen us to be his possession. We are the thing that he wants out of this great work of redemption.

We are God's possession. Peter is pressing home the great truth that God takes delight in his people, and that we are the objects upon which he has set his love and affection and delight. It is almost embarrassing, isn't it, to feel that delightful gaze of God? Do you remember when you first knew the love of your husband or your wife? Your spouse looked at you, and there were times when you almost felt embarrassed that somebody loved you so much. You almost had to turn away from him or her, because this person was delighted to look at you, delighted to talk with you, and delighted to be with you. Peter is saying, *I want you to think about it, Christian. God has put his gaze of delight upon you. He sets his love on you.*

Jesus prays for our grasp of God's love in the great high priestly prayer of John 17, that we would share that love with him and the Father, which they shared with each other from before the foundation of the world. I would be a heretic in saying this if Jesus had not said it first: The Father does not love you less than he loves his own Son.

C. H. Spurgeon once said, "When you look at the cross, you have to ask the question, does He love us more than He loves His own Son?"[7] Peter is pressing home that God has taken delight in his one people, and, therefore, because God delights in his people, we are to live our lives declaring the excellencies of his mercy to the nations, living distinctly from the world, and bearing witness to his holiness with our lips and our lives. That is what it means to be the one people of God.

---

[7] As C. H. Spurgeon used to say, "Whenever we gaze at the cross, we ought to be constrained to say, 'Does He love *me* more than He loves *Him*? That he would give *Him* for *me*?'" Sinclair Ferguson, *Something to Boast About*, sermon delivered at First Presbyterian Church, Jackson, MS, January 30, 2005.

6

One Way

D. A. CARSON

"Enter through the narrow gate. For wide is the gate and broad is the road that leads to destruction, and many enter through it."

MATTHEW 7:13[1]

I am sure you have occasionally followed the editorial pages of a newspaper when people are writing on religious matters. Particularly during some controversy, someone will sooner or later say, "I could put up with those Christians if they just followed Jesus a little more. I mean, in the Sermon on the Mount, Jesus says, 'Turn the other cheek,' and things like that. But all these Christians do nothing but condemn other people."

Sometimes painful experiences lurk behind these complaints. Christians are not always consistent. For all our claims about loving God with heart and soul and mind and strength, and our neighbors as ourselves, too frequently our integrity breaks down. Of course, some heated resentments against Christians spring less from Christian failures than from the very nature of Christianity: its claims to be exclusive can be very irritating in a pluralistic age. And inevitably, the two issues frequently become confused in the minds of outside observers who have had rather mixed experiences with

---

[1] Unless otherwise noted, Scripture references quoted in this chapter are taken from the *New International Version* of the Bible (NIV).

actual Christians. Embarrassed by the criticisms, even some Christians join their critics and begin to ask the question, Does Christianity really demand one way of life in contrast with all others?

Sharp Antitheses: Two Ways

Since critics often measure Christians against Jesus' Sermon on the Mount, let us begin there. One of the first things a careful inquirer finds is that the Sermon on the Mount is anything but simplistic. The same Jesus who says, "Do not judge, or you too will be judged," also says, "Do not throw your pearls to pigs"—which means somebody has to figure out who the swine are (Matt. 7:1, 6). The same Jesus who says "Turn . . . the other [cheek]" (Matt. 5:39) adds, at the end of the Sermon on the Mount, some startlingly antithetical things. Particularly in the last section, Matthew 7:13–29, Jesus casts four striking antitheses: two ways, two trees, two claims, and two foundations. In each instance, there are but two possibilities, there are only two ways, one of which is right and the other wrong.

First there are two ways: "Enter through the narrow gate. For wide is the gate and broad is the road that leads to destruction, and many enter through it. But small is the gate and narrow the road that leads to life, and only a few find it" (Matt. 7:13–14). According to Jesus, God's way is not spacious. It is in some sense confining and relatively unpopular. Only a few find it, we are told. This is not meant to suggest that there aren't millions and millions of redeemed on the last day (look at the book of Revelation!). It does mean that this is the common appearance of things in this world, for in most contexts Christians are vastly outnumbered by unbelievers. Inevitably, the Christian way is viewed as narrow, restricted, dense, and unpopular.

Next, Jesus speaks of two trees: "Every good tree bears good fruit, but a bad tree bears bad fruit. A good tree cannot bear bad fruit, and a bad tree cannot bear good fruit. Every tree that does not bear good fruit is cut down and thrown into the fire. Thus, by their fruit you will recognize them" (Matt. 7:17–20). On first reading, this seems simple enough: one tree produces good fruit and another tree produces bad fruit. But Jesus sets this antithesis in a context which makes it much more challenging. He is concerned with false teaching in the church: "Watch out for false prophets. They come to you in sheep's clothing, but inwardly they are ferocious wolves. By their fruit you will recognize them" (Matt. 7:15–16).

It is tough enough to make your way in this world and try to defend the truth of the Scriptures, the glory of Christ, and what the cross is about to people who are completely outside, or who are completely opposed to the gospel, people who have no Christian heritage at all. But it is all the more difficult when we consider the situation within the church. Here we find people who in some sense have understanding of Christian terminology and Christian commitments, but who are subtly steering away from what is central in favor of what is at best peripheral. Initial evaluation demands that we be charitable, so we hopefully affirm, "Oh, yes, here is a brother, a sister." But then we listen more attentively to what they are actually saying, and we stop and think, *Is this right? Does this square with Scripture?* Suddenly, we discover that the most dangerous teachers are not the ones who are on the outside, but the ones who are on the inside of the church—the ones who are respected, privileged, informed, well-educated, seminary trained, and who certainly display all our forms of piety. If you begin to question them, they say, "I'm a Christian, just like you." Aren't they the hardest ones to handle? For at least in some instances, we may not even be sure we are right in our negative assessment. We wonder, am I just too narrow, bigoted, right wing, and old-fashioned?

Of course, this is nothing new. When the apostle Paul addressed the Ephesian elders, he warned them that from their own number some would arise as ravenous wolves to destroy the flock.

In the Sermon on the Mount, Jesus himself says, "Watch out for false prophets. They come to you in sheep's clothing" (Matt. 7:15). They wear the right clothes, and they sound like sheep, complete with appropriate bleats. But watch out for those teeth! It is within this context that Jesus says that we can finally distinguish them by their fruit.

The trouble, of course, is that fruit often takes a long time to grow, and we want instant discernment. Wouldn't it be nice if every single movement that came along was either stamped *Made in Heaven* or *Designed in the Pit*? Then you could bless it or damn it and get on with life. But rarely do movements arise with such clear identity. They may have a veneer stamped *Made in Heaven*, but inwardly they may be dangerous and destructive. It may take quite a long time before the fruit finally emerges and shows the reality for what it is. By then how many generations of young or uninformed Christians have been influenced or even stamped by these errors?

Two ways, two trees, and now two claims. One claim seems very religious, pious, and spiritual. Many say, "Lord, Lord." But Jesus insists that it's not the one who says, "Lord, Lord" who enters on the last day but the one who does the will of his Father in heaven. Moreover, it's not a matter of verbal claims alone, but of conduct. "Many," Jesus says, "will say to me on that day, 'Lord, how can you possibly exclude us? I preached and preached. In fact, I've been endowed with the gift of prophecy, and I've done all of this in your name. Indeed, in your name I've cast out demons. In your name I've performed miracles. And you tell me now I can't get in? If anybody's qualified to get in—well, I mean, I've done all of this in your name, Jesus'" (Matt. 7:22, author's paraphrase). But still Jesus will tell them plainly, "I never knew you. Away from me, you evildoers!" (Matt. 7:23). No, the only one who enters, we are told, is the one who does the will of Jesus' Father who is in heaven.

Then comes the last of these four vignettes: two foundations.

One person builds his house on solid rock that can withstand any of the storms of life while the other builds on sand. When a violent storm assaults these two houses, the first remains immovable. The ground on which the second is built turns into a quagmire, and the building itself turns out to be about as stable as certain hillside homes in California (see Matt. 7:24–27).

Now what are we to make of all of this? Is this realistic? Why must we choose between a narrow gate with a small, narrow road, and a broad gate with a wide road? How about an in-between road—not too narrow, not wide and relativistic, but sort of in-between? How about trees that produce things that Garrison Keillor would deem "pretty good"? He offers us "pretty good" poems and an entire catalog of "pretty good" stuff. Surely he is the sort of person who would prefer trees which, while they may not produce either crab apples or honest-to-goodness New Zealand Gala apples, nevertheless yield pretty good apples. Will that do? Isn't this the way we want to operate? "Yes, I know there's a certain amount of inconsistency in all of us, but, Lord, it must count for something that we've actually preached in your name and in your name dispatched demons. Admittedly, I have committed some sins, but how about the fact that I am principled and obedient a lot of the time?" Will that do? Is it really a choice between solid rock and sand? How about hardpan clay?

Yes, but . . .

In fact, if we find such sharp antitheses difficult to live with, we need to remind ourselves that the Bible itself multiplies such antitheses. In one sense, therefore, the more biblically we think about these sets of sharply defined ways—one right and the other wrong—the more we find ourselves warned to be careful.

Many passages offer the sharpest antitheses, not least in the Old Testament. Deuteronomy, for example, says, "I call heaven and earth as witnesses against you that I have set before you life and death, blessings and curses. Now choose life, so that you and your children may live" (Deut. 30:19). And there are texts like Psalm 1, sometimes called a *wisdom* Psalm, which offers only two ways to live:

> Blessed is the man who does not walk in the counsel of the wicked or stand in the way of sinners or sit in the seat of mockers. But his delight is in the law of the LORD, and on his law he meditates day and night. He is like a tree planted by streams of water, which yields its fruit in its season and whose leaf does not wither. Whatever he does prospers. (Ps. 1:1–3)

That's the good side. But verse 4 takes up the antithesis: "Not so the wicked!" Everything fundamental that you can postulate of the righteous, you must deny to the unrighteous. Do the righteous avoid the counsel of ungodly people? Not so the wicked! Do the righteous avoid the lifestyle, the way of living and conduct, of ungodly people? Not so the wicked! Do the righteous avoid a condescending, sneering mockery? Not so the wicked! Do the righteous love the Word of God, such that they delight in it and meditate on it day and night? Not so the wicked! Are the righteous like a tree that puts down its roots and is always showing signs of life, always green and full, and in due course produces fruit? Not so the wicked!

Well, what are the wicked like? They're like the chaff that the wind blows away, we're told—lifeless, fruitless, rootless, unstable, insignificant—an absolute antithesis to the living and fruitful tree. Indeed, the psalm ends with one final and devastating antithesis: "The LORD watches over the way of the righteous, but the way of the wicked will perish" (Ps. 1:6).

The contrast presented in these passages could not be more sharply antithetical. But the reflective reader of Scripture responds, "Yes, yes, I hear these principles. I see that this is taught in holy Scripture. But do not the actual histories of biblical people show that the antitheses of these texts need to be somewhat attenuated? Is it not the case that most people produce some good fruit and some bad fruit? Do not believers in the Bible commonly alternate between rock foundation and sand, between the narrow way and the broad? For instance, what about David? He was a man after God's own heart, mightily praised, yet he ended up committing adultery and murder. What about Abraham? Yes, he was called "a friend of God," and he is the ultimate patriarch. Yes, he is the archetypal man of faith. But at the end of the day he is also a liar. And then there's the great patriarchal family. One of them is sleeping with his daughter-in-law, and another is sleeping with his father's concubine. Ten of them are trying to sell the eleventh into slavery, unless they decide to murder him instead. And these are the patriarchs!

For further evidence, we might adduce Peter. Jesus says, "Blessed are you, Simon son of Jonah, for this was not revealed to you by man, but by my Father in heaven. And I tell you that you are Peter, and on this rock I will build my church" (Matt. 16:17–18). Immediately, Peter tries to give Jesus a theology lesson and urges him not to die on the cross! Then on top of all of that, despite being warned off, Peter manages to swear and insist that he never met Jesus and with foul language disowns him entirely. Even after Pentecost Peter gets his theology wrong in Antioch and has to be rebuked by another apostle (Gal. 2:11–14).

Only two ways to live? "Give me a break," people respond. "Wouldn't it be better to speak of a spectrum?" Even believers are sometimes good, sometimes bad. Isn't that what you find in your own life? So where do these antitheses come from? Why is Jesus' language so sharp?

A Closer Look

We had better look a little more closely at these antitheses from the Sermon on the Mount. Start with the structure of the sermon, and thus how it fits together. My father used to tell me that a text without a context becomes a pretext for a proof text, so when I was still quite young I learned to look at the context.

The Sermon on the Mount runs through Matthew 5, 6, and 7. The body of the sermon, the heart of the passage, runs from 5:17 to 7:12. It's marked by what is sometimes called an *inclusio*—a kind of literary marker, a bracket at the front end and at the back end—that resonates with the same words or themes and says, "This is what I'm talking about." The front of an inclusio tells us, "This is what I will be teaching"; the back says, "So that's what this was about."

The body of the Sermon on the Mount begins with Jesus' statement in Matthew 5:17: "Do not think that I have come to abolish *the Law or the Prophets*; I have not come to abolish them but to fulfill them." Then, in Matthew 7:12 Jesus concludes: "So in everything, do to others what you would have them do to you, for this sums up *the Law and the Prophets*." Within this inclusio, Jesus has a great deal to say about the kingdom, but the inclusio itself alerts the reader to that fact that the Sermon on the Mount relates Jesus' teaching regarding the kingdom to the Law and the Prophets. The Sermon on the Mount is about this: Jesus announces and describes the kingdom of heaven as the fulfillment of earlier Scripture, of the law and the prophets.

But before the body of the Sermon on the Mount begins in Matthew 5:17, we find the Beatitudes (Matt. 5:3–10), which give us what some have called the "norms of the kingdom." Have you noticed the blessing promised by the first Beatitude? "Blessed are the poor in spirit, *for theirs is the kingdom of heaven*" (Matt. 5:3). The last of these Beatitudes promises the same reward: "Blessed are those who are persecuted because of righteousness, *for theirs is the kingdom of heaven*" (Matt. 5:10). Here, then, is another simple *inclusio*, another literary marker. We must understand that the Beatitudes treat the kingdom of heaven; they provide the norms of the kingdom. This is what the kingdom of heaven looks like. This is the way people in the kingdom of heaven act. The last beatitude is then expanded to warn us about persecution for those who live in this way (Matt. 5:11–12). We are to live as the Beatitudes prescribe—as salt and light in this fallen, dark, and decaying world (Matt. 5:13–16).

The Beatitudes provide the introduction to the Sermon on the Mount, followed by the Sermon's body that explains what the kingdom is and does, and how it fulfills the Old Testament anticipation. After this body of instruction, when we come to the very end of the Sermon on the Mount, we find the antitheses that we have already surveyed. Two ways to live—just two ways—the narrow way or the broad way: that's the first antithesis. Producing good fruit or bad fruit: that's the second. Our claim before Jesus is backed up by either character and conduct or just empty words: that's the third antithesis. Then we have the fourth: building on rock or building on sand.

How on earth are we to live this out? To answer rightly, let us now nestle the Sermon on the Mount within the whole flow of the Gospel of Matthew. Matthew, like all four canonical Gospels, can be described as a passion narrative preceded by a long introduction. That is, all of the Gospels—the biblical Gospels at least—are stories about Jesus' ministry on his way to the cross and resurrection. They convey the good news of Jesus going to the cross.

This reminds us of the real reason that *The Da Vinci Code*, which depends for its argument on a lot of late "gospels," and the recently unearthed *The Gospel of Judas*, which has garnered so much attention, are such nonsense. I mean that in the strictest sense of the word: historically speaking, as *gospels* they are nonsense. A great deal of the argumentation in *The Da Vinci Code* depends on late second- and third-century gnostic documents, including one called *The Gospel of Philip*. There is nothing wrong with that title, except that by first-century standards it's not a gospel, and in any case it's not by Philip. Apart from that the title is pretty accurate! You see, a gospel in the first century was bound up with the "good news" of Jesus Christ. In the first century they didn't speak of four *Gospels*; they spoke of "*the* Gospel according to Matthew," "*the* Gospel according to Mark," "*the* Gospel according to Luke," and "*the* Gospel according to John."

There is just one gospel. This one gospel of Jesus Christ, attested by the first four books of the New Testament, has certain essential features. The gospel is the account of what Jesus came to do, climaxing in the cross and the resurrection. What permits us to call each of these first four books of the New Testament *a* Gospel is that it presents *the* gospel—the good news of Jesus Christ, born among us, serving, teaching, preaching, healing, transforming, announcing, inaugurating his kingdom and, finally, going to the cross himself as a ransom for many (Mark 10:45; Matt. 20:28). On the night that he was betrayed, he explained that the blood that he was shedding is the blood of the new covenant. By the second century, each of these four books came to be called *a* Gospel because it so faithfully conveyed *the* gospel.

But the books that were written at the end of the second century and in the third century, which called themselves *gospels*, clearly failed to understand the derivation. So when I read something like *The Gospel of Thomas*, which consists of 114 sayings (there are only two tiny snippets of ostensible history in the entire document) or *The Gospel of Philip*, I see that it is not properly called a *gospel* at all. Rather, it is what later gnostic heretics put in place of the gospel because they do not want the cross and the resurrection. They want wise utterances that we can "know," so that if you have this "knowledge," this *gnosis*, then you have an inside track to spirituality. But what they offer is not the gospel at all.

The gospel is the good news that Christ Jesus came to save sinners by his life, death, and resurrection—to save them not merely from condemnation but from the practice of sin. We are saved from everything loaded with rebellion against God: the performance and habits and self-deceit of sin, the wretched idolatry that dethrones God, and all the condemnation and enslavement that accrue because of such anarchic rebellion. We are not saved because we have learned some wise sayings. We are saved because Jesus is the king, and his unutterably powerful reign undoes evil and will one day transform this broken world into the new heaven and the new earth, the home of righteousness. We are saved because he is the high priest, perfectly mediating between the holy God and his sinful image-bearers. We are saved because he is the prophet: he perfectly brings the Word of God, and he is himself the Word of God. He inaugurates the kingdom, and in the Sermon on the Mount he shows us what must characterize this kingdom: no hate, no lust, no deceit, no lying. That is why Jesus sets forth his kingdom norms in the Sermon on the Mount: he has already inaugurated the kingdom.

Already in measure the followers of Jesus Christ—those who have been healed by him, forgiven by him, and transformed by him—are to reflect these priorities. These are the norms of the kingdom. These constitute kingdom ethics.

At the end of the day, there are only two ways—the way of the kingdom or the way of death. But still, we cannot save ourselves by obeying the Sermon on the Mount. This is why Christians have always recognized that the Sermon on the Mount simultaneously tells us how to live and exposes us to the fact that we cannot meet the challenge. It probes us deeply and shows us our inconsistencies and our double standards. Yes, do not commit adultery: perhaps we can manage that. But Jesus tells us we are not even supposed to lust. Suddenly we do not know where to hide our shame. Do not commit murder: fine; most of us will manage a passing grade on that one. But Jesus insists we are not supposed to hate. Again, we are so ashamed that we do not know where to look. Then Jesus comes to the end of his exhortations and says, "There are only two ways: one is right and leads to life, the other is wrong and leads to death." The four antitheses leave us no place to hide.

Let me tell you frankly: if the Gospel of Matthew ended after chapter 7, I would be in despair. But the kingdom that Jesus comes to inaugurate is more than a batch of moral instruction. Its power is bound up with Jesus' death and resurrection on behalf of his people, and all the transformation of individuals that flows from that death and resurrection. That's why in the book of Acts, in the earliest records of the post-Pentecost believers, when Christians describe themselves as "followers of the Way," they ultimately mean that Jesus is the way. After all, that is what Jesus explicitly taught: "I am the way, the truth, the life. No one comes to the Father except through me" (John 14:6). It turns out that we're not going to succeed in following the Way if the Way is nothing more than our righteousness and our consistency. There is a "way" of life we must follow, yet ultimately Jesus himself is the Way, and that's why the apostle Peter, after the death, resurrection, and exaltation of Christ, could pronounce that there is salvation in no one else, for there is no other name given to us under heaven by which we must be saved (Acts 4:12).

The Sermon on the Mount sets forth the starkest challenge. After all, at the end of chapter 5, Jesus says, "Be perfect . . . as your heavenly Father is perfect" (v. 48). If that's the standard, I'm done. But then we read further in Matthew's Gospel, "It is not the healthy who need a doctor, but the sick. . . . I have not come to call the righteous, but sinners" (Matt. 9:12–13). And then Jesus goes to the cross.

Do you know the New Testament book that sets out this tension most dramatically—this tension between the demand for perfection, the insistence that we must have perfection before God, and the frankest recognition that we are not a perfect people? Do you know which book it is? It's 1 John. After the initial paragraph that introduces the book, John begins by insisting in the strongest language—and he's writing to Christians—that if anyone says he doesn't sin, he's a liar. The truth isn't in him. If anyone says he hasn't sinned, he's kidding himself. It's worse than that. Such a person is actually calling God a liar because God says that we do sin. He's kidding himself, he's not telling the truth, and he's calling God a liar, because the fact of the matter is that we sin; God says we do (1:10). The proper solution, John says, is not to deny that we commit sin; rather, the proper solution is this: "If we confess our sins, he is faithful and just and will forgive us our sins and purify us from all unrighteousness" (1:9). That's the solution. In short, John comforts us by reminding us we have an Advocate with the Father, Jesus Christ, the Righteous One, who is the propitiation for our sins (1 John 2:2).

But the tension can be from either end. For just when we think that such freedom and grace in the gospel guarantee a carefree passage, we are told that if we don't believe the truth—certain definite truths about Jesus—we're not in. Then John says that if we are not obedient to Christ, if we do not bow the knee before him morally, we are not in. If we do not love our brothers and sisters in Christ, we are not in. The language gets stronger and stronger until we come to these shocking words, "No one who is born of God will continue to sin, because God's seed remains in him" (3:9). A Christian cannot go on sinning because he has been born of God. I know all the arguments about what a Greek present tense means and how a Christian might not *go on sinning* but sin once in awhile, but isn't that peeling the onion pretty fine? In short, John's moral commandments seem to exclude people like me.

What do we do with this? In the light of a book that has already begun by saying, "We are all going to sin," it is helpful to remember that the word *cannot* does not always provide us with an ontological impossibility. It does not always mean something that cannot possibly be. Sometimes it provides us with a moral imperative.

Let me give you an example. When I was a lad in school, in

grade seven, we had a teacher who had been in World War II in the Canadian army. He wished, I think, that he were still in the army, and we did, too. He was not God's gift to teaching. He thought that students would and should and could obey him exactly the way soldiers would obey a drill sergeant. Understandably, he found it very difficult to control a classroom.

Now, if there was one thing he loathed with a passion, it was gum chewing. If he found somebody chewing gum, he would pick up the rubbish can by his desk, hobble down the aisle, stand beside that student, and stick the dustbin right under the student's nose. Then with all his limited eloquence he would solemnly intone:

A gum-chewing boy and a cud-chewing cow
Look so much alike, yet different somehow.
What is the difference? Ah, I see it now:
'Tis the thoughtful look in the face of the cow.

And then he would shout, "Spit!"

What was Mr. Cooper telling this miscreant? This ritual was, in fact, a way of informing him and the rest of us in the class, "You cannot chew gum here." What I want to point out is that even then I realized that it would have quite missed the point if I had lifted my hand in the third row and said, "Mr. Cooper, ontologically speaking, you're mistaken. You say I cannot chew gum here—but I'm doing it!" For in reality, Mr. Cooper was not stating an ontological impossibility; he was expressing a moral imperative. The words *You cannot chew gum here* mean, in this context, "You *must not* chew gum in class! If you do, you are out of line and will be in big trouble."

This is the very way the Bible sets out two ways. There is one right way and one wrong way, the wise way and the foolish way, the godly way and the ungodly way, the narrow way and the broad way. The Bible speaks with an absolute antithesis: You cannot sin here. Sinning is not done here. Sinning is always without excuse: you cannot sin here. It quite misses the point to say, "Well, ontologically speaking, you're mistaken; I'm doing it." Sinning is *not* done here. Yet John has already recognized in his first chapter-and-a-half that, God help us, we do sin here.

In fact, Jesus Christ died for sinners. He bore our sins in his own body on the tree; his sacrifice turns aside the righteous wrath of God, and Jesus himself remains our advocate and high priest forever. He has poured out his Spirit upon us as the down payment of the full inheritance yet to come. Although we are not yet in the consummated glory—not yet in the new heavens and the new earth, where we really will not sin at all—already, right now, among Christ's people, it has been declared, "You cannot sin here. Sinning is not done here." And when, poor, frail, creatures that we are, we do sin, we return to the one place where there is hope: the cross of Christ. On the one hand, we desperately need the absolute antitheses so that we learn resolutely not to make excuses for our sin; on the other, we need the frank candor of the biblical histories to remind us that God, rich in mercy, while never for a moment diminishing the splendor of his holiness, accepts poor sinners still. For such tension, there is only one resolution: the cross, the cross, always the cross.

One Way: Jesus Christ

So we are driven back to the cross again and again and again:

> *Nothing in my hand I bring,*
> *Simply to thy cross I cling;*
> *Naked, come to thee for dress;*
> *Helpless, look to thee for grace;*
> *Foul, I to the fountain fly;*
> *Wash me, Savior, or I die.*

For, you see, if the antitheses of Scripture remind us that there are two ways to live, they also tell us that there is only one way to God. At one level we can say it is the way of righteousness. But because we are sinners still, our only way forever remains the one who said, "I am the way and the truth and the life. No one comes to the Father except through me" (John 14:6). *Except through me.*

Scripture Index

General Index

ALLIANCE®
OF CONFESSING EVANGELICALS

The Philadelphia Conference on Reformed Theology (PCRT) is the oldest, national, continuous Reformed conference in the United States. Founded by Dr. James Boice in 1974, PCRT has continued to thrive and grow. Initially held only in its titular city, PCRT now takes place in four different cities across the nation. An enduring legacy of the Alliance of Confessing Evangelicals, this conference has taken its place among those ministries that have fostered renewal in the church.

The Alliance is a coalition of Christians from various denominations (Baptist, Presbyterian, Reformed, Congregational, Anglican, Lutheran, etc.) committed to producing and promoting resources for a modern reformation of North America's churches in doctrine, worship, and life according to Scripture.

The Alliance carries out this mission through its broadcasting, events, publishing, and Reformed resources. Alliance broadcasts included: *The Bible Study Hour* with Dr. James Boice, *Every Last Word* featuring Dr. Philip Ryken, *God's Living Word* with Bible teacher Rev. Richard Phillips, and *Dr. Barnhouse & the Bible* with Dr. Donald Barnhouse. The programs can be heard throughout the United States as well as online.

Events such as PCRT help spread the mission and message of the Alliance to people everywhere. The Alliance also sponsors many regional events including reformed theology conferences, pastors' conferences, and Reformation Society meetings.

reformation21, the Alliance's online magazine, is only one of our many publishing projects, both online and in print. We also publish *God's Word Today* online daily devotional; Alliance booklets with a list of diverse authors; *Today's Issues* booklets in partnership with Crossway Books; and more.

Lastly, the Alliance seeks to encourage reformation in the church today by offering a wide variety of audio resources to our friends and donors. You can buy CDs featuring Alliance broadcast speakers and many other pastors and theologians including Alistair Begg, Mark Dever, Ligon Duncan, R. C. Sproul, and David Wells.